WOMEN RISKTAKERS

It's Your Destiny—
Reach Higher
Stand Stronger
Go Further

by

Dr. Patricia D. Bailey

Harrison House
Tulsa, Oklahoma

09 08 07 06 05 04   10 9 8 7 6 5 4 3 2 1

Women Risktakers:
It's Your Destiny—Reach Higher, Stand Stronger, Go Further
ISBN 1-57794-527-1
Copyright © 2004 by Dr. Patricia D. Bailey
Master's Touch Ministries International
P.O. Box 3175
Alpharetta, Georgia 30023

Published by Harrison House, Inc.
P.O. Box 35035
Tulsa, Oklahoma 74153

Contents

INTRODUCTION:
THE LEAP OF FAITH

Throughout history, God has used women to fulfill many of His most strategic purposes. The women in the Bible whose examples we glean from in this book all took risks to become women of purpose. Each of these role models adhered to specific attributes and overcame fear or another hindrance in order to press through and complete her God-ordained destiny. The risks each took were based on one common risk, the one God wants us to take today.

Everything we do for God requires a risk, and everything we do for God costs us something through the most important medium of exchange in our possession—faith. Hebrews 11:6 (NIV) says, "Without faith it is impossible to please God…," and James 2:20 plainly tells us, "…faith without works is dead."

Faith is simply moving out on God's statements in His Word, the Bible. By faith, we risk everything we own in favor and pursuit of the fulfillment of God's Word and His promises in our lives. When we take a risk by moving out in faith, is the risk really a risk? Or is it a leap of faith?

The hidden treasures and endless potentials that lie within every woman are buried beneath the initiative to launch into action. This book is designed to challenge you and ignite your faith, to encourage and show you how to take the action needed to fulfill your destiny!

Sometimes in life in order to take the leap of faith, we must face and confront the habits, fears, or any other hindrances constraining us.

What fears are keeping us bound in a fruitless pattern or cycle that our lives have set in place for us up to this point? Where are we allowing procrastination to entrap us? Are we looking to people to validate and sanction our future and our dreams? What and who are the influences in our lives that we allow to sway us negatively? We must learn how to stop taking our dreams before dream killers by sharing our 11 x 16 visions with people who have had only 5 x 7 visions and experiences!

We must believe in God *and* in ourselves. Trusting in God is not a risk. He has never failed but has proven Himself throughout the ages to be trustworthy. We need approval and sanctioning from God alone. The opinions of human beings, who may not sanction our God-given dreams, do not matter. God is the One who created a specific destiny for each of us and provided Himself as the means to fulfill it, for those of us who will believe in and receive His Son, Jesus.

When you develop an intimate relationship with Jesus, the Shepherd and Bishop of your soul,[1] when you discover the power that lies within you, the collaboration of your partnership with Christ Jesus makes you more than a conqueror.[2] No obstacle is lethal enough to erase the potential that you possess.

What are the demands on your life that you've allowed but God has never required of you? What past failures have you allowed to obscure your view of your God-ordained future? What condemnations have you let plague and influence you, even to the point of falsely determining that you may have little value as a person, that you may not merit the blessings that people of worth are allowed?

Rather than focusing on overcoming weaknesses, this book highlights your potential and the need to fulfill it so that you develop an insatiable desire to launch out into your destiny—and not even wait until tomorrow, but begin today. Of course, this book is also a book of principles. It teaches you how to create atmospheres that are conducive to the realization of your dreams.

My emphasis in this book is on the importance of giving more attention to the finality of God's Word rather than to the opinions of men. The women whose lives we examine each took the common risk that changed their world of simply taking God at His undeviating Word. There really isn't a risk when we dare to trust God because He always causes us to triumph in Christ Jesus.[3] With man some things are impossible, but with God all things are possible![4]

Our victories don't come without obstacles, but God gives us the faith to overcome all of them.[5] Our successes don't come without temptations, but God gives us the way of escape from each one.[6] God watches every single motion of our lives with detailed observation. Nothing is hidden from His sight. He watches over our lives to bring us to the completion of the work that He has begun in us.[7]

Follow the Course by Faith

In order to arrive in the appointed place at the appointed time, sometimes we have to make mid-course corrections. We can see an analogy in the method used to plan and control the path of a space flight.

A spacecraft's course is carefully planned before the launch by taking a number of conditions into consideration. Although the "trajectory projection" is precisely calculated to propel the spacecraft into the orbit or orbits it will assume on the way to its destination, the flight path will still require adjustments and corrections after launch. How well we know that in life the course we have planned to take to our destination will require adjustments and corrections along the way as well!

Some adjustments we make by confronting the obstacle that is hindering us from traveling in the right direction or even on the right path; some we make by listening and following God's directions. Other adjustments God makes. In working together conditions of which we are unaware, if we are walking the course by sight rather than by faith,[8] we may feel that God is moving us in a direction that our human minds may think is the wrong one, even the opposite way we should go to fulfill our destiny. In the spaceflight analogy, a spacecraft's trajectory is sometimes projected in a direction opposite to its destination. The primary goal in determining the course is not to calculate the shortest distance but to minimize the amount of fuel needed. Otherwise, the cost of fuel would be prohibitive.

Time of launch and use of the earth's rotation, the gravitational pull of the earth, sun, moon, and other bodies, in addition to more obvious factors such as speed and distance, are among multiple factors calculated to minimize the fuel requirement and project the trajectory. Someone unaware of the many underlying goals and conditions calculated to project the best, rather than the most direct, course to the destination would wonder why the spacecraft was being launched in the "wrong direction."

When God leads us along the course in a direction away from completing goals we would have set if we had made the plans, we must continue to follow the course He has projected and adjusted for us, knowing that His ways are higher than our ways, and His thoughts are higher than our thoughts.[9]

As we follow God, sometimes we wander off course. But in spite of our faults and imperfections, God orchestrates our lives so that we land on the mark He desires for us. Even if you feel it's too late to fulfill your God-given dreams, this book is for you. In the plan God destined for us before time began, He factored in all our experiences—victories *and* failures. He factored in the times we became frustrated while waiting and stepped out ahead of Him, the times of disobedience, and the time required for restoration in order for us to get back on course. He slows our progression down just enough to accommodate our hasty anxieties.

He factored into His plan for our lives the times when we were let down by leadership and quit going to church out of disappointment and the times we entered wrong relationships then went through a healing process before we could trust again. He calculated into our course the times we entered a season of fear and failed to trust Him and the times some of us who failed to trust Him with our tithes and offerings fell behind, ensnared financially.

He projected our life's trajectory and calculated into it our life experiences for us to reach His predetermined place of assignment, predestined according to His purpose, the purpose of the One who works out everything in agreement with the counsel and design of His own will, in His own way.[10] He makes us complete in every good work to do His will, working in us that which is well pleasing in His sight and established by Him and for Him before time ever began.[11] Then when we complete the course in spite of our failures and diversions, He receives the glory. We can give Him the honor and praise due Him for His never-failing, never-ending, unconditional love for us.

A new life awaits you. Within you is the initiative to take the leap of faith into that new life. This book will unlock the treasure of potential, purpose, and power that resides within you. Deposited in you before time ever began, that treasure will enable you to risk nothing by risking everything for the future God has promised you!

Get off the vicious cycle of repetition and mediocrity. Take the risk, the leap of faith, by taking God at His Word.

Part 1

Hagar:
The Paradox
of Submission

1

THE WAY UP WAS DOWN!

Hagar, an Egyptian maidservant, took the risk of submitting her will to the will of the Lord and, as a result, came to receive an inheritance from the Lord that profited the generations that followed.

Being at the mercy of someone else's selfish ambition, Hagar experienced the greatest magnitude of agony and ache. But even more, Hagar's plight demonstrated God's ability to work for good an onslaught of events seemingly sent by the enemy to derail a life.

To those who have been betrayed, used, or abused and are trying to find self-value in the midst of despair, it may not seem possible that any good in life can ever come out of such pain. To those who have been struggling, trying to find worth in the midst of pain and despair from the most lethal weapon of all, rejection, it may not seem possible that victory could come out of such defeat or that God could bring forth life out of death. In the example of Hagar, the slave girl with no rights and no voice, from ancestors whose traditional religion was Egyptology, we see how the majestic God moves. So magnificent that He had no one greater than Himself to swear by in giving Abram the covenant promise,[1] He also wants to be intricately involved in our lives to pull us out of those painful traps and launch us into our destiny and purpose.

Hagar learned well God's ability to turn pain into purpose. And in Hagar's reliance on God, we also see a demonstration of His most interesting ability: to birth a sense of purpose out of our greatest mistakes. Both Hagar, as maidservant to Sarai, and Sarai made mistakes that God birthed into purpose.

The Promise

God promised Abram:

In your seed all the nations of the earth shall be blessed, because you have obeyed My voice.

Genesis 22:18 NKJV

Sarai was the blessed wife of Abram—the man of great wealth,[2] the man to whom God had decreed He would make a great nation whose seed would be as innumerable as the dust of the earth or the stars of the heaven or the sand on the seashore, and in that seed all the nations of the world would be blessed[3]—except that Sarai was childless! There was not yet an heir from whom the great nation could come that God had promised Abram.

Sarai became impatient waiting for God to fulfill His promise to Abram and took matters into her own hands, victimizing Hagar.

It had been more than a decade since God had given Abram the mandate to leave the place of his birth and travel to a place God appointed, a fertile place where God would fulfill His promise to Abram.

...Get out of your country, from your family and from your father's house, to a land that I will show you.

I will make you a great nation; I will bless you and make your name great; and you shall be a blessing.

I will bless those who bless you, and I will curse him who curses you; and in you all the families of the earth shall be blessed.

Genesis 12:1-3 NKJV

The place the divine compass directed Abram where God could finally unfold the purpose He had for Abram's life was Canaan.

Then Abram took Sarai his wife and Lot his brother's son, and all their possessions that they had gathered, and the people whom they had acquired in Haran, and they departed to go to the land of Canaan. So they came to the land of Canaan.

Then the LORD appeared to Abram and said, "To your descendants I will give this land." And there he built an altar to the LORD, who had appeared to him.

Genesis 12:5,7 NKJV

Abram dwelt in the land of Canaan....And the LORD said to Abram..."Lift your eyes now and look from the place where you are...for all the land which you see I give to you and your descendants forever. And I will make your descendants as the dust of the earth...."

Genesis 13:12,14-16 NKJV

God promised Abram all the land he could see and, as He did in the other times He renewed His promise to the childless Abram, spoke of Abram's innumerable descendants. God's promise was too big for any human being to abort or contaminate with opinions and philosophies. Although Sarai was visualizing the manifestation of the promise with difficulty, Abram continued to evoke the

3

promises of God by holding fast to the words of God as we see in Genesis 15:6: "And he believed in the LORD; and he counted it to him for righteousness."

No Sign of the Promise

The ten years had come and gone since Abram and Sarai had begun dwelling in the land of Canaan, the place of promise, without any sign of the fruit of the promise having come.[4] It was then that Sarai decided to take matters into her own hands.

As everyone waited for Abram's promised child to arrive, Hagar went about completing her routine duties as Sarai's maidservant. We can imagine the details of their daily lives. Sarai had trained Hagar very well. Her role and assignments were very clear, and she learned to live to please her mistress. She knew how Sarai liked her food prepared, her clothes laundered, and her tent tied. Her mistress's every wish was Hagar's command.

In this role, Hagar became familiar with Sarai's joys and struggles. Month after month, Hagar witnessed Sarai's agony in waiting for the evidence of the promise. Perhaps Hagar even consoled Sarai, saying, "Mistress, don't worry. Your time will soon come."

Hagar likely was younger than Sarai and solemnly observed the effects of gravity and time raging against her mistress's lifelong dream of becoming a mother. At the same time, Sarai must have noted not only Hagar's faithful and dependable servanthood, but also her youthfulness, strength, and maidenhood. Noting these qualities, she forged an unthinkable plan, which we find in Genesis 16:2 (NKJV):

So Sarai said to Abram, "See now, the LORD has restrained me from bearing children. Please, go in to my maid; perhaps I shall obtain children by her." And Abram heeded the voice of Sarai.

How often in life have we all done something like Sarai did? We know beyond any doubt that we have a particular promise from God. In times past we have seen His mighty outstretched hand. Yet in the midst of our stand of faith waiting for this promise, we experience the enemy constantly trying to pressure us from every side. He tempts us simply to doubt with the aim being to bring anxiety and selfish ambition into our lives. He tempts us with impatience and fear hoping to bring us to the point of taking matters into our own hands to try to make the promise come to pass.

The paralysis of fear blinds us to our past victories in God. Before long, if we yield to the enemy's entrapment, our view will be obscured by despair and the ache of inadequacy. The danger in this is the risk of compromise. And what we compromise to gain, we will always lose.

Sarai compromised by rationalizing that the way the promise could be fulfilled would be by following a custom of the East, which was not considered to be dishonorable or immoral in polygamous countries. The childless wife would give her slave maidservant to her husband for the specific purpose of conceiving and giving birth to an heir whom the wife would adopt.[5] That custom was not for Abram and Sarai to follow, however! That action displayed a lack of trust that God would perform the promise, and they soon began to experience the consequences of trying to bring the promise to pass their way.

The Counterfeit Sacrifice

When Sarai beckoned to Hagar and gave Hagar her next assignment, Hagar must have been completely taken aback. "She wants me to lie with her husband?" Hagar's mind must have raced. "She wants me to bare the promised seed? What will my master say to this request?"

From the biblical account, we cannot see whether Hagar was reluctant to comply with Sarai's request. It is possible that she viewed this assignment as an opportunity to move closer to her wealthy master. But more than likely, she quietly and reluctantly submitted, perhaps having seen a glimpse of Sarai's wrath and being afraid to reveal her reluctance.

As Sarai drew Abram and Hagar into her plan, she pulled them into her disobedience. This is the tragedy of taking matters into our own hands. How blinded we become to others' needs and rights when we allow selfish ambition and impatience, rather than faith, to rule our lives! These compulsive behaviors are simply fear disguised as zeal, and patient faith must replace them if we are ever to see the manifestation of the promise we await. Sarai's impatience will result in a counterfeit sacrifice to the promise that God will refuse to alter.

A Desperate Plan

Regardless of Hagar's feelings, Sarai in her desperation took the maidservant to her very own husband. And exactly according to Sarai's plan, Hagar conceived a child.

Then the tide turned. When Hagar discovered that she had conceived, the Bible says that she despised Sarai.[6] As a result of Hagar's apparent disrespect for her mistress, Sarai asked Abram for permission to deal with her.

Then Sarai said to Abram, "My wrong be upon you! I gave my maid into your embrace; and when she saw that she had conceived, I became despised in her eyes. The LORD judge between you and me." So Abram said to Sarai, "Indeed your maid is in your hand; do to her as you please...."

Genesis 16:5,6 NKJV

Contrary to Hagar's expectation, Sarai rejected her rather than appreciated her for carrying out her own request. In essence, Hagar had been raped, not by Abram, but by Sarai's selfish ambition. Sarai had used Hagar for her own purposes, and when Hagar's physical compliance did not produce the desired emotional reward within Sarai, Sarai rejected her.

Escape

Bewildered by Sarai's rejection, Hagar made the mistake of allowing her pain to navigate her in the direction of her past.

...And when Sarai dealt harshly with her, she fled from her presence.

Genesis 16:6 NKJV

Hagar must have thought, *How could she be bitter towards me? After all, I am pregnant because of her desire and her request! My life was interrupted without my permission!* She ran in fear instead of dealing with what had happened. In running from confronting the past, she was on the verge of jeopardizing her future.

An Angelic Visitation

In the wilderness, miles away from Abram and Sarai, Hagar agonized over Sarai's cutting actions. Her story, however, was about to take an amazing turn. In the middle of her lonely, self-imposed exile, this Gentile Egyptian maidservant became the first woman to be visited by an angel!

> *Now the Angel of the LORD found her by a spring of water in the wilderness, by the spring on the way to Shur.*
>
> Genesis 16:7 NKJV

God Himself delivered His word of instruction to this outcast, forsaken, and rejected woman. Even though Hagar's ancestors had worshipped every god imaginable except Him, Jehovah's eyes were upon her. During Hagar's loneliest moments, He was with her, and He knew very well the meaning of her name.

Hagar means "flight,"[7] and she was surely marked and plagued by the impulse to flee. Like so many who have sought love, acceptance, and fulfillment in all the wrong places, she lived a life of constant flight from one journey to the next.

God knew Hagar's tendency to run. He sent His messenger to tell her, "Hagar, Sarai's maid, where have you come from, and where are you going?" (v. 8 NKJV).

He needed her to slow down. He must have been softly speaking to her words similar to those of the song artist India Arie:

> Slow down, Baby you're going too fast
> You got you hands in the air
> With you feet on the gas
> You're 'bout to wreck your future
> Running from your past....

In the midst of Hagar's desert, God provided a spring. In her emotional and spiritual wilderness, God provided a well of comfort. But the pain and rejection Hagar ran from almost blinded her to the springs of comfort and instruction brought by the messenger of God.

The Appointed Place

The spring at which God's messenger met Hagar was a road map leading the way to Shur. Hagar must have been planning to flee back to Egypt by way of Shur. *Shur* in the Hebrew language means "a wall."[8] Shur was "east of Egypt,"[9] "even as far as the land of Egypt."[10] Hagar, in fleeing toward Egypt, in the sense of running toward the safety of her homeland, her past, was running right into a wall.

The place where Hagar came to the end of herself depicts the work that was being done inside of her. Anxiously running from what she should confront to what, in her mind, was the better destination, the safety of her homeland, Hagar paused in her desperate flight in a place that spoke to the very core of her existence. The skillful Master had her in the palm of His powerful hand and had placed her in that significant place.

God is so personal, detailed, and specific in His plans for us. In His plan for Hagar, He had foreordained the space and time at which she would stop in her race of denial and escapism. He had already accurately measured her level of endurance so that at the time when she would come to the end of herself she would be at a spring on the path to Shur. Rather than running from what she should confront into the dead end of trying to return to the safety of her past, she would reach a place that would bring forth new life.

God, who is eternity future and eternity past, monitored Hagar's comings and goings. How awesome is the God of Hagar! God, the only true and living God with whom no one can compare, whom no other god is beside, the everlasting King[11] who sits enthroned above the universe, wants to be intricately involved in our lives. How well Hagar was coming to know this!

Return and Submit

In this appointed place, Hagar responded to the question God's messenger asked her. When Hagar told him, "I am fleeing from the presence of my mistress Sarai" (v. 8 NKJV), he instructed her, "Return to your mistress, and submit yourself under her hand" (v. 9 NKJV).

The angel reminded Hagar that she was still Sarai's maid. Hagar had an unfinished task: She had not departed from her master correctly. It was not yet her season for departure.

One sure thing in our personal walk with God is that we cannot move out prematurely. Many times we seek a way out of a difficult situation, not realizing that God is trying to work valuable character traits within us. He is at work in our lives "both to will and to do for His good pleasure."[12]

Hagar had risen up with pride against Sarai when she had discovered she was with child. Although Sarai's request had been contrary to God's will, Saria was still Hagar's mistress. Hagar was to submit to serving and fulfilling the request of her mistress. Because God wanted to expose this sin in Hagar's life, He mandated her return to the place of her disobedience to confront her pride and pain. He instructed her to submit.

Sometimes dying a deeper death to self is more painful than we care to endure, but each day we must place our ambitions, desires, and longings before the Master. We must make a daily altar in prayer and in the Word of God, which instructs us to present ourselves as living sacrifices, holy and acceptable to God. This is our "reasonable service."[13] We are not required to be acceptable to any human being (not even to ourselves), but to God alone (through *His* righteousness we come boldly before His throne, acknowledging the areas where we have missed the mark, approaching Him in desperate need of restoration). In other words, our "reasonable service" is the *least* that we could do.

Any sacrifice we make for the Master is not acceptable until our hearts are yielded to His will and way. Psalm 51:17 (AMP) tells us that the sacrifice acceptable to God "is a broken spirit; a broken and a contrite heart [broken down with sorrow for sin and humbly and thoroughly penitent]...." The Father wants us to approach Him with a contrite heart, reaching with outstretched arms to Him, living broken before Him in the sense of being ready to admit our mistakes and shortcomings to Him, completely open for Him to help us. The Father wants to help us. He has a destiny for us that will exceed the expectations of any we could plan for ourselves. And to be able to do everything He wants to do for us and through us, He wants our daily dependency to be on Him, daily submitting to His will.

Isaiah 57:15 (NKJV) tells us that "the High and Lofty One who inhabits eternity" dwells "with him who has a contrite and humble spirit, to revive the spirit of the humble, and to revive the heart of the contrite ones." God ordered Hagar's steps in her flight from her painful past. When Hagar came to the end of herself as a broken and contrite spirit before God, He began creating within her a strong dwelling place for Himself and for His plan.

A deeper relationship began developing between Hagar and her God. In her wilderness, God was doing a work by a spring and bringing forth a new birth through her humbled heart for the purpose of a bountiful harvest for Him.

A Word of Promise

When the angel appeared to Hagar, it is likely that the last words she expected to hear were to go back to her pain and rejection!

The Greek word translated *contrite* in Isaiah 57:15 is from a word meaning "crushed" to "powder."[14] This must have been how Hagar, contrite and humble, felt as she began her journey to Sarai, whose harsh treatment of her was the very reason she had fled to the wilderness in the first place.

As her steps drew ever closer to the city limits of Canaan, the force of Sarai's rejection must have slowed her every step, but the words of the angel continued to prompt her onward. Hagar had received not only a word of instruction, but also a word of promise. Genesis 16:10 (NKJV) records the Lord's promise to her:

> ...*I will multiply your descendants exceedingly, so that they shall not be counted for multitude.*

This is the promise of innumerable descendants that God had given Abram! In her obedience to God to submit and return to her mistress, Hagar was tapping into the promise God gave Abram. God was birthing mistakes into purpose!

From Pain to Promise to Purpose

The promise comes only after obedient submission. Could it be that often we seek a blessing without meeting the prerequisite of submission? When we submit ourselves under the hand of God, humility flourishes, and this is when God will exalt us.[15] If we contend to pursue life from the perspective of doing things God's way, we will get God's results. When Hagar was obedient to go back to the place that was torment for her, she tapped into God's promise that would yield the results He intended. The key to God working positively in the situation was in Hagar taking the risk to trust Him and submit to His instructions. She submitted to confronting the fear from which she had run in order to move forward with Him.

God had promised to multiply Abram's seed beyond measure, and Sarai would carry the seed that God had chosen to fulfill and proclaim His ultimate covenant. However, God in His mercy sent His angel to encourage and comfort Hagar by acknowledging the seed within her. God did not dismiss the seed in her womb as if it were not Abram's. The promise belonged to Hagar as well.

> ...*"Behold, you are with child, and you shall bear a son. You shall call his name Ishmael, because the LORD has heard your affliction."*
>
> Genesis 16:11 NKJV

The eyes of God were upon Hagar to guide her through her situation as Psalm 32:8 (NKJV) says: "I will guide you with My eye." Hagar could feel His telescopic eyes piercing through her pain and rejection and healing her soul. This encounter reshaped her life, and God's strength gave her the boldness to take the risk of returning to her mistress.

13

After Hagar made the decision to submit and return, we can see how her relationship with the Lord began to deepen. The care and delicate, detailed attention the Master gave her built her self-esteem and strengthened her step.

Hagar had been privileged with something that not even Sarai had experienced—she was the receiver of a special message from God Himself; the Creator of heaven and earth honored her with an angelic visit. She could never have imagined that her flight from the presence of her sorrow could have afforded her an invitation into His presence. In the presence of the Lord there is fullness of joy.

Regardless of the situation, it is amazing how our perspective on life totally changes when we spend time in the presence of our holy God.

Hagar's Gift to God

Hagar desired to give God something in return for the gift of His visitation, but what could one give the Master? The position and mindset of servitude were familiar to her, but how did one serve the Creator of the universe? Ultimately, she reached within and found a gift for God: a name.

> So she called the name of the Lord Who spoke to her, You are a God of seeing, for she said, Have I [not] even here [in the wilderness] looked upon Him Who sees me [and lived]?
>
> Or have I here also seen [the future purposes or designs of] Him Who sees me? Therefore the well was called Beer-lahai-roi [A well to the Living One Who sees me]; it is between Kadesh and Bered.
>
> Genesis 16:13,14 AMP

This Gentile maidservant dared to give God a name! She was not a priest, prophet, or king, but God bestowed value on her and embraced this name. God values those who are dispensable to others. This rejected one was not only the first woman to be visited by God's angel, but the first person to give Him a name!

A maidservant took the risk of giving the Creator a name henceforth affirming His faithfulness and compassion. Hagar gazed upon the One who saw her, the One who sees the beginning and the end. One translation of Genesis 16:13 states: "Hagar gave a name to Yahweh who had spoken to her: 'You are El Roi,' for, she said, 'Surely this is a place where I, in my turn, have seen the one who sees me?'" (JB). "El Roi"—the God who sees the high and mighty and the meek and low—had seen Hagar, a maidservant fleeing from her pain and frustration.

The well, the appointed meeting place, now "Beer-lahai-roi [a well to the Living One Who sees me]" stood between Kadesh and Bered. *Kadesh* means "holy"[16] "sanctuary,"[17] and *Bered* means "hail."[18] God saw Hagar between the holy place and the storm in her life. Holy means a cut above the raised standard. God recruited Hagar to go the extra mile, to turn the other cheek, and to give more than she felt she could offer.

The Paradox of Submission

Submission is not submission until we are asked to do something that we really despise doing. Everything within Hagar detested the thought of submitting to Sarai. Genesis 16:6 (AMP) tells

us that "…Sarai [had] dealt severely with her, humbling and afflict-
ing her.…"

The paradox of submission is a riddle of intrigue. The way up
is down. The way to success is in humbling oneself under God's
mighty hand. The more humility one possesses, the more God is
able to trust that person in an exalted position.

Hagar's life demonstrates for us this self-sacrificial process of
humility, and her decision to obey provoked the blessings of inheritance. Submission always precedes the blessing.

Why Us?

Hagar must have asked, "Why me?" hundreds of times. Have
you ever asked this?

I'm writing to the wife who feels that it is impossible to submit
one more day to that insensitive husband. I'm writing to the corporate woman who is paid to submit to that unsaved male chauvinist
boss, before whom God has appointed her to demonstrate His
character, and to the woman who is submitting to someone in leadership less qualified than she is. All are asking, "Why me?"

I'm writing to the woman who is in despair over betrayal or
rejection, asking, "Why me? How do I find worth and self-value in
this?" and to the woman experiencing physical abuse who is not
only asking, "Why me?" but needs immediate permanent relief
from the abuse or a way to place distance between her and the
abuser. (God's requirement of submission does not include submitting to physical abuse.)

The answer to, "Why me?" is this: God is at work in the midst of the situation in us and through us to make us vessels equipped for His use—for His purpose and grace.[19] He is at work in us to mirror His express image, "the exact representation of His being,"[20] Jesus, into the various situations to which He has assigned us. God will work in all situations, even in circumstances caused by Satan or human choice or frailty, to turn them to the good for those who love God and are called according to His purpose.[21]

It is important to emphasize that God does not cause abuse or place sickness or disease upon us to help us grow. He wouldn't plague us with an illness after Jesus died upon the cross to purchase our healing[22] (as well as to take our sins upon Himself). He uses the circumstances to help us grow in attributes such as submission. Learning how to hear and obey Him is extremely important. He uses circumstances to help us exercise our faith and grow in patience and in the other fruit of the Spirit needed to fulfill the assignments He has given us.

God is working intricately in our lives to equip us in order for us to fulfill a bigger and better destiny than we could ever imagine. When we submit to the Master, His powerful hand holds, consoles, shapes, and then molds us into the vessels that He desires, giving us worth, value, and purpose again.

A Great Advantage

As God moved in Hagar's life, and the lives of others of the Old Testament times, He will move in our lives today, but we have a great advantage! After the fall of man, when man chose to rebel rather than submit to God's instruction, sin separated man from God. After this event, we see God interacting with mankind by coming upon, speaking to, or appearing to man through different means, communicating and empowering man from the outside, throughout the Old Testament. With the New Covenant, Jesus came to earth and died on the cross for our sins and iniquities and was resurrected by God to provide the Way[23] for God, in all His power, to live inside us.

Galatians 3:16 (NKJV) tells us, "Now to Abraham [Abram] and his Seed were the promises made. He does not say, 'And to seeds,' as of many, but as of one, 'And to your Seed,' who is Christ." Galatians 3:29 (NKJV) tells us, "And if you are Christ's, then you are Abraham's seed, and heirs according to the promise."

When God spoke the promise to Abram, He gave him a mandate that He would bless him and his Seed. The Seed of Abram is Jesus. Those who believe in Abram's Seed, Jesus, The Way to God, are grafted in as heirs of God's promise to Abram.[24] Those of us today who choose to be grafted in are among the blessed seed as innumerable as the dust of the earth or the stars of the heaven or the sand on the seashore that God promised Abram.

When we accept and believe the work Jesus did for us to restore our relationship with the Father, the eternal godhead[25] comes to live inside us, inside our frail human vessels, giving us all the power to rule and reign on the earth that the Father originally intended for man before the fall.

This means we are not defenseless against the grip and entrapments, the onslaughts, the enemy uses to try to overcome us. God will continue to work in us, vessels that will never reach perfection on earth, but will also work through us to manifest His power on earth.

God has already given us everything that pertains to life and godliness and has begun a good work inside us that He will complete. He will be with us and won't forsake us regardless of how distant He may appear to be. He is a very present help here with us in our time of need. Our job description is to continue to keep our eyes upon Jesus and stir up the gift of God in us, stir up ourselves in the Holy Ghost. God never demands anything *from* us that He is not willing to provide *to* us.[26]

We must encourage ourselves in the Lord. He has provided for us. *We* can fulfill our assignments! We can make it; we can achieve it; *we can do it!* Whether we believe it or not, we already have what it takes to pass the test. We are stronger than we think we are. He will never overload us; He never places more on us than we can bear. He knows the extent of our load of saturation and wants us to keep our dependency on Him in carrying out our assignment.

A paradox of submission is that the more we, in our frail human vessels, yield ourselves to the Lord by daily submitting to His will, the stronger dwelling place for Him in His glory we become and the greater measure of His power we are able to release into the earth as part of His plan for us.

2

THE HIGH PRIZE
FROM SUBMISSION

Notice that as Hagar spent time in God's presence, the angel of the Lord did not condemn her past or weaknesses. Instead, his words aimed her expectations toward something greater than her own selfish needs. This desperate mother had aspirations for the posterity of her offspring. With the type of stubborn determination that only a mother possesses, Hagar anchored her faith in the prophetic promise of the Lord to increase her seed. A sense of comfort and hope began to arise in her heart as the Lord through the angel spoke a word into her future.

This life we live is much bigger than us. God has orchestrated it in such a way that our daily dependence has to be on Him alone in order to yield the fruit we need—"love, joy, peace, longsuffering, kindness, goodness, faithfulness, gentleness, self-control"[1]—to fulfill our purpose.

As we draw nearer to Him, God draws nearer to us.[2] Then at some point, we find our wills submitting to His will. A portion of His will is deposited into our hearts, and His desires somehow become our desires. Only God knows how long it will take for us to make this exchange of our wills for His, but soon we find ourselves pleading for His will. Then our prayers will begin to reflect our Savior's: "Not My will, but Yours, be done."[3] This is how God's will is accomplished here on earth as it is in heaven.[4]

The pregnant and growing Hagar took the optimum risk to return to Abram and Sarai to face the fire. She took the risk of trusting God and submitting to Him by going back into a situation she would not otherwise have wanted to face. Sometimes the hardest thing to do is to return to the place of adversity and confront our fears, weaknesses, and most often the source, or sources, of our intimidation.

A new day dawned as Hagar returned to the compound of Abram. As she saw it in the near distance, she must have felt herself weakening under the pressure mounting within her. As she approached the place of her torment while feeling the effects of her pregnancy, she must have reminded herself over and over of the promise of God concerning her son.

As the time of the baby's birth drew near and Hagar felt the sharp pains of contractions becoming closer and closer, and as the piercing pain intensified, and then her water broke and she began to deliver, with every fervent push she must have gripped the words of her Master, the One who saw her, the One who was at all times alert to her faintest cry.

With the final strength within her, she bent forward to push for the last time, the baby's head protruded, then seconds later the baby's gender was confirmed. It was a boy: a beautiful, dark-haired, olive-skinned baby boy. There was no question of the baby's name because God Himself had named him: "The Angel of the LORD said to her: '...you shall bear a son. You shall call his name Ishmael....'"[5] As Hagar held him, she said, "Ishmael. Your name is Ishmael. God Himself named you."

Little did Hagar know that the birth and life of Ishmael would impact the predestined course and flow of history. The child, as innocent as he was, now signified the very essence of a self-willed act.

A Self-Willed Act

Sarai's impatient, self-serving act had produced Ishmael ahead of God's promised child. Impatient, self-willed acts will never produce the promise.

Because God has given each of us the privilege of a will, the luxury of choice is a significant component affecting the outcome of our lives. Our eternal God can see into the future what we could never see, so daily He woos us to Himself to enable us to make choices according to His will. Through our encounters with Him, He increases and we decrease.[6] We cannot enter the manifested presence of God and leave self-absorbed.

In her self-absorption, Sarai was unwilling to allow the virtue of patience to have its perfect work.[7] The completion of the perfect work enables us to maintain the covenant blessing we obtain. It takes faith to receive the promise God has ordained for us, and it takes patience and character to maintain what He has given us.

Despite our self-willed acts, God somehow achieves His sovereign plan. He will never alter the things that come out of his mouth.

His words are forever established.[8] Heaven and earth will pass away, but His Word will never pass away.[9]

Hagar's Submission

After Ishmael's birth, although Abram was legally and economically responsible for him, his mother Hagar was still viewed as Sarai's property. Hagar knew that her role was to aid, assist, and serve her mistress and did so for the next more than fifteen years.

Everything within Hagar screamed to hold on to her self-will. However, submission is what God desired from her, and submission is what He desires from each of us.

The Bible instructs us on the topic of submission:

Servants (slaves), be obedient to those who are your physical masters, having respect for them and eager concern to please them, in singleness of motive and with all your heart, as [service] to Christ [Himself]—not in the way of eye-service [as if they were watching you] and only to please men, but as servants (slaves) of Christ, doing the will of God heartily and with your whole soul; rendering service readily with goodwill, as to the Lord and not to men.

Ephesians 6:5-7 AMP

Just when we want to say, "I didn't do anything to deserve this!" we need to look at 1 Peter 2:19 (AMP):

For one is regarded favorably (is approved, acceptable, and thankworthy) if, as in the sight of God, he endures the pain of unjust suffering.

Liberation is found in submission. Submission truly is our aid, not our enemy. If there has ever been an attribute that has been misinterpreted and disguised wrongfully, it is submission, but when we see the effect of submission on our souls, it is no wonder why God prizes it so highly.

Submission cuts like a laser the cancers from our souls. It demands that we eradicate all selfishness that has taken root in our lives from birth to adulthood and exposes our lifelong intents and motives. When it reveals deceit, it commands it to bow! Submission exposes our schemes, plots, and plans, and forces us to forgive, love, and esteem others higher than ourselves.

New Names, Renewed Vision

Although Abram was eighty-six years older than Ishmael,[10] we can imagine that father and son developed a strong bond during Hagar's years of silent submission.

When Abram was ninety-nine (and Ishmael was thirteen), God visited Abram and commanded him to walk blamelessly before Him.[11] Abram fell on his face, and God reminded him of His covenant promise and knighted him "Father of Many Nations," changing his name to Abraham.[12]

Then God told Abraham His expectations of him and his seed after him:

…"As for you, you shall keep My covenant, you and your descendants after you throughout their generations.

"This is My covenant which you shall keep, between Me and you and your descendants after you: Every male child among you shall be circumcised; and you shall be circumcised in the flesh of

your foreskins, and it shall be a sign of the covenant between Me and you."

Genesis 17:9-11 NKJV

After instructing Abraham with the details of the requirements of circumcision, God addressed the topic of Abraham's wife, Sarai:

…*"As for Sarai your wife, you shall not call her name Sarai, but Sarah shall be her name.*

"And I will bless her and also give you a son by her; then I will bless her, and she shall be a mother of nations; kings of peoples shall be from her."

Genesis 17:15,16 NKJV

God Did Not Forget Ishmael

Abraham's response illuminates his feelings, not only about Sarah becoming a mother, but toward his thirteen-year-old son, Ishmael.

Then Abraham fell on his face and laughed, and said in his heart, "Shall a child be born to a man who is one hundred years old? And shall Sarah, who is ninety years old, bear a child?"

And Abraham said to God, "Oh, that Ishmael might live before You!"

Genesis 17:17,18 NKJV

God clearly told Abraham that Ishmael was not His predestined perfect plan. Isaac, the baby to be born of Sarah, was the promised child.[13]

However, God did not forget His promise to the woman who took a risk and gave God a name. His eyes were upon her seed for good. While speaking with Abraham, He confirmed what He had already told Hagar:

"And as for Ishmael, I have heard you. Behold, I have blessed him, and will make him fruitful, and will multiply him exceedingly. He shall beget twelve princes, and I will make him a great nation."

Genesis 17:20 NKJV

In obedience to God's instructions, Abraham took his son, Ishmael, and all of his male servants to be circumcised. Together, father and son were circumcised and went through the process of healing, which must have strengthened their bond even more.

The Bitter Arrival of the Promised Son

Finally, Sarah conceived and Isaac was born. Ishmael, accustomed to being his father's only son, now had a sibling to contend with. The personal attention formerly given to him alone would now have to be distributed between him and his brother.

Genesis 21 records the outcome of this conflict:

So the child grew and was weaned. And Abraham made a great feast on the same day that Isaac was weaned. And Sarah saw the son of Hagar the Egyptian, whom she had borne to Abraham, scoffing.

Genesis 21:8,9 NKJV

The proud mother, Sarah, wanted this day to be perfect, for it marked not only her son's maturing but the end of a miraculous nursing relationship between her nearly hundred-year-old self and her promised child. By no means did Sarah intend to share this day with Hagar and Ishmael.

Verses 10-11 (NKJV) tell the story:

Therefore she said to Abraham, "Cast out this bondwoman and her son; for the son of this bondwoman shall not be heir with my son, namely with Isaac." And the matter was very displeasing in Abraham's sight because of his son.

With the shift in attention, Ishmael began to mock Isaac. The severity of the mockery is not made clear in the biblical account. Perhaps it was the normal teasing that happens between brothers, but however extreme, it was perceived by Sarah as something more, possibly because of her own contention with Hagar. That the two women did not share a harmonious relationship is clear.

"Cast out this bondwoman and her son," Sarah had said. Abraham knew what this request would mean. The words cut like daggers into the core of his heart. Ishmael was not only the son of "this bondwoman" but of Abraham as well. For more than fifteen years they had grown in their relationship, and now Sarah was asking him to abandon his own offspring, his own seed!

The Master Plan

As harsh as this request seemed, it housed the integrity of God's sovereign plan for the nation of Israel. This did not mean that the promised child was better than the self-willed child. The master plan of God is not an issue of supremacy of roles; He has chosen all of us. However, the Master had made an irrevocable covenant with Abraham and his seed through Sarah.

The difficult task awaiting Abraham disheartened him, but he could not just ignore Sarah's request to send Hagar and Ishmael away, for the Lord Himself affirmed Sarah's words.

…"Do not let it be displeasing in your sight because of the lad or because of your bondwoman. Whatever Sarah has said to you, listen to her voice; for in Isaac your seed shall be called."

Genesis 21:12 NKJV

Abraham was about to face the most difficult task he had ever been given. Ishmael, Abraham's seed and firstborn son, represented his worth and, if not for Isaac, would have secured his name and inheritance. But most of all, Abraham loved and cherished Ishmael.

No One Could Change His Plan

Hagar heard Sarah's harsh request, and after more than fifteen years of submission, she faced rejection and abandonment once again. She must have wondered, "God, how could You be in agreement with Sarah? What about Your promise to me?" Hagar's heart was broken, but God could not alter His plan.

No emotion or action could change what God had willed before the foundation of the earth. Before Sarah had ever conceived her self-willed plan, God had already started a course in history of a legacy that would pass through Abraham.

When God first decreed His covenant with Abraham that we read about in Genesis 12:1-3, it is possible that Sarah may not have been completely aware of the oath or its meaning. Or, Sarah may have understood but did not have faith even then that it would come to pass through her.

God spoke to Abraham of the covenant several more times during the next twenty-five years until Isaac's birth. God told Abraham the heir would come from Abraham's "own body,"[14] but

God didn't specifically name Sarah as the one who would give birth to the heir of the covenant until after Ishmael was born. Shortly after God told Abraham when Ishmael was thirteen that Sarah would bear him a son to be named "Isaac" and God would establish His covenant with him and his descendants,[15] Sarah herself heard God speaking of the covenant to Abraham and naming her as the one to bear the heir, "…Sarah your wife shall have a son."[16]

Regardless of her intent or reasoning behind her decision to follow her own plan, Sarah was not in submission to God's direction. We don't usually have all the information our human minds would like to know before taking the "risk" of faith in obeying God, nor do we know the way our destiny will fit into God's greater plan.

Just as we see in Hagar's example God's design to bless through our submission to Him, we see in Sarah's example the negative results that flow out of such an unsubmissive act when we decide that our plan will work better than God's. With the information we have now, we know He has established His plan since the beginning of time. The same God that was there for women who had less to work with than we do, is the same God that we serve today.

Sarah's disobedience in diverting God's plan by her selfish, ambitious plot that resulted in the birth of Ishmael did not change God's plan. God had already established in heaven before time began and on earth through the covenant promise He had given His representative and vessel, Abraham, His will for Israel and intent to work through Abraham and Abraham's son Isaac born to Sarah.

The child produced from Sarah's plan was not the heir God intended to fulfill the covenant.

God Did Not Forget Ishmael

Nothing could change God's plan, and nothing is powerful enough to thwart God's redemptive power, but our merciful God saw the dilemma Abraham faced in sending away his firstborn son.

Observing Abraham's anguish, God sent him a word of comfort. God assured Abraham that He would take care of Hagar and Ishmael:

> ..."Do not let it be displeasing in your sight because of the lad or because of your bondwoman....I will also make a nation of the son of the bondwoman, because he is your seed."
>
> Genesis 21:12,13 NKJV

This word eased Abraham's apprehensions over the welfare of Ishmael, and Hagar as well. The Lord's word to him enabled him to move out in confidence. And that's all we ever need to step out in faith for any difficult issue that we face. The Word of the Lord is sure and final. We can find our security in anchoring our lives upon His Word regardless of the way circumstances appear, or if the direction of the trajectory He has projected for us is opposite to the way our minds think we should go. No matter what difficulties and delays we experience, our great stabilizer is our dependence upon the Lord and His Word.

Abraham knew to set his mind to keep his thoughts in line with the word of the Lord to him as he prepared to submit to God's instructions. What thoughts did Abraham have to bring under subjection in order to comply by sending Hagar and Ishmael away? Early the next morning, before doubt had a chance to alter the course of his day, Abraham fulfilled the request of God. He gave Hagar bread and skin water and sent the two away.[17]

Be assured that we, too, will face difficult assignments from God, and everything within us may reason and pull against what is clearly commanded of us. But 2 Corinthians 10:5 tells us that we must bring every thought into captivity to the obedience of Christ, to the Word of God.

Silent Submission

As we study this account, it is hard to begin to imagine what Hagar was thinking as Abraham delivered their teenaged son over to her and sent the two away! The Scriptures do not suggest that this man of great wealth gave her any money. He did not assign any of his servants to escort her. How unimaginably cruel and insensitive this must have seemed to Hagar!

Even though we know the background that sending Hagar and Ishmael away was very displeasing to Abraham and that God reassured him, the biblical account portrays an emotionless Abraham sending the two away and a submissive Hagar departing without a word.

From Hagar's perspective, Abraham's actions alone screamed, "Rejection!" Among her initial flurry of thoughts must have been this one: *"Not again—here I am fleeing once again!"* The first time she had run away on her own accord, but this time her master was sending her away. She could not rebel against her master's orders; there was no possibility of her returning. A bondwoman didn't have rights. She had no grounds to complain or rebuke the actions of Abraham and Sarah; she didn't even have a right to her own opinion.

If there had ever been a time when she must have wanted to express how she felt to them, this had to have been the occasion. However, her choice to respond through submission and obedience outweighed the pain of rejection, and she quietly took her son and departed.

There are times in our lives when we need to make the decision to depart in silence. We need to just let the situation go and think, *Good-bye; it's time to move on.* We often miss the opportunity to celebrate the invitation of our future and destiny because we are mourning what we have to leave, but what we need to do is simply depart and not look back.

Even when the departure is not a pleasant one, just move on. If a relationship has ended against your will, move on. Every person has the ability to change his or her mind. God is the only constant. One change of mind can crumble your life and destiny if you allow it to. But when people change, you also have the prerogative to change and transition into the next phase of your life. Move out and move on. As painful as it may be, just depart; don't look back; get over it—move on! This doesn't mean to run from a situation God wants you to stay in, as Hagar did, but when the season and assignment from God is over, *it's over.*

Sometimes we want to offer that last uttered opinion before we move on. That's what gets us in trouble. It's a wonderful thing to have an opinion, but when our opinion competes with God's work of submission, we have to silence it until the appropriate time.

Many of us have experienced the negative effects of succumbing to that feeling of urgency to have the last word or the feeling of pressure to make our point. Some of us, after unwisely offering an opinion, have lost one of the most valuable relationships we have ever had, ended a marriage, or lost a job! Then we and our strong opinion go to lunch alone, spend Christmas alone, and spend life alone because nobody else wants to keep company with us and our mighty opinion.

It seems a small matter to open or close our mouths as we please. However, James 3:6 (NKJV) illuminates the true force of such self-willed speaking: "The tongue is a fire, a world of iniquity. The tongue is so set among our members that it defiles the whole body, and sets on fire the course of nature; and it is set on fire by hell."

Keeping our mouths closed gives us strength to submit. When we offer a strong opinion without thinking instead of closing our mouths in submission, the poison that comes out will set us back every time. How many times have we said something out of anger, only to regret it later? Words are eternal. They never die.

It is our human nature to crave to defend ourselves. It's called self-preservation, the law of nature. Yes, it may be the law of nature, but it certainly isn't the law of God! Remember, submitting to God provokes the blessings of inheritance.

3

FROM REJECTION TO PURPOSE

As Hagar, twice rejected, walked into the scorching desert with her son, her easiest response would have been to give up. The sand blowing in the hot desert winds, her son's confused and hurt questioning, her own dry breath—every sound echoed contrary to her promised destiny.

On her nomadic journey, Hagar wandered and perhaps wondered with the constant question, *Where do I go from here?* producing more aimless wandering. At that moment, Hagar had to choose whether to become bitter or to allow the situation to make her better. The biblical account does not describe her attitude, but we do know that she was resolved to continue on the journey set before her. She never tried to run back to Abraham to seek refuge, knowing that the season of her life with Abraham and Sarah was over.

Each step of the way, Hagar had a promise to hold on to. Her first visitation from God had been so real to her that no one could talk her out of her promise or cause her to deny it. The encounter had made her a woman of strength.

A Woman of Strength

There is a vast difference between a strong woman and a woman of strength. The strong woman places her confidence in her own strength. The woman of strength realizes that she can do all things only through Christ who strengthens her.[1]

A woman of strength is true to herself. She is aware of her weaknesses, yet she chooses to live beyond her limitations. She does not dine at the table of defeat. She "does not eat the bread of idleness," but her "delight is in the law of the LORD," and she "meditates it," feasts upon it, "day and night" to make it her ultimate "schoolmaster," companion, guide, and eternal lamp to her path.[2] On a day-to-day basis, regardless of the opposition, she observes to do all that is written therein, and she has learned that the Master makes her way prosperous as she observes to do all that He commands.[3]

This is the definition and confession of a woman of strength, and this was who Hagar had become. Though her journey had launched her into a state of wandering, the compass to guide her was a God who had already seen her established end.

Clinging to Life

Hagar's departure from her son's father had left her disoriented by rejection. Her spirit had been crushed, yet her will to survive was fueled by her son's need for her to live.

The battle with the intense heat of the desert, the need for water, and the diminishing food supply competed with her resolve to survive. We know that with a mother's love for her son, she would have forfeited satisfying her own thirst to pour the final drops of water from the skin into the mouth of weary Ishmael. She needed him—the promise of her future, the contender for the covenant, the beneficiary of the promised inheritance. Yet the skin was as empty of water as was her hope for security and direction.

Wandering, constantly plagued with wondering, *Where do I go from here?*—the outcome of her present situation and the pressure to make the right choice weighed heavily upon her thoughts. She desperately clung to life, not only for herself, but for her son.

Perhaps as she considered losing him, she remembered the times of Ishmael's jovial laughter and play. Ishmael was the part of her life she had pride in, her first real accomplishment, something she proved that she could do well, and now every natural element seemed poised to destroy him.

At night they had no place to go for shelter or safety from the freezing chill of the desert, leaving them chilled to the marrow of their bones. Hagar attempted to warm Ishmael with her own cold, malnourished body.

"I Will Not See Him Die"

For Hagar, all hope seemed lost.

...in the Wilderness of Beersheba...the water in the skin was used up, and she placed the boy under one of the shrubs. Then she went and sat down across from him at a distance of about a bowshot; for she said to herself, "Let me not see the death of the boy." So she sat opposite him, and lifted her voice and wept.

Genesis 21:14-16 NKJV

Rather than watch her son die, Hagar made the most difficult decision of her life. She had nothing to give him anymore: no food, no water, no hope, and no direction. She put her teenaged son under a shrub and walked away from her pain, her problem, and her future.

Many of us have had similar experiences in our own lives. Your desert may not be sand dunes, but your present circumstances may appear just as barren and lifeless. You may be facing a seemingly desperate situation, but don't give up! Remember: You are never alone. The righteous are never forsaken. They never have to beg for bread.[4]

Even in Hagar's moment of seeming hopelessness, she spoke a word of hope: "Let me not see the death of the boy." Although most likely Hagar was expressing her fear of seeing him take his last breath, her words positioned her for a miracle. By saying, *"I will not see him die!"* that is exactly what she received.

God Heard

God heard Hagar's faith-filled request. Of the millions of requests that daily reach heaven's throne room, each one receives detailed and explicit attention. Thank God, He's not like emergency room paramedics, whose attention must be directed based on the severity of the problem. Rather, our Master gives the same beautiful attention to the prayer of the first-grader learning his multiplication tables as He does to the prayer of the child whose mother is fighting cancer.

He commits Himself to His loving plan for all humankind. He hears, He sees, He knows, and He is daily touched by the feeling of our infirmities.[5]

In the midst of Hagar's desperation, God stepped in right on time and proved to be her very present help in her time of trouble.[6]

And God heard the voice of the lad. Then the angel of God called to Hagar out of heaven, and said to her, "What ails you, Hagar? Fear not, for God has heard the voice of the lad where he is."

Genesis 21:17 NKJV

The Voice of Her Son

The Bible says that as Hagar wept before the Lord, God heard the voice of her son crying.[7] Likewise, as you cry out to God, He will hear the inner cry of your child. Even if your child is wandering in the dark away from Him, seemingly empty of everything you have poured into your son's or daughter's life, God will hear your child. His eye is ever upon your children for good.

May this comfort the mother whose child is in jail, on drugs, or in rebellion: God hears your child where that child is! May this comfort the mother who has not heard a word from her child in years: God hears your child where that child is!

You have a prophetic promise in Isaiah 49:15 that He will not forsake you. Neither will He forsake your offspring.[8] God says that He will make good His promise to you and to your children after you.

Arise!

When God had gotten Hagar's attention, He continued to encourage her:

"Arise, lift up the lad and hold him with your hand, for I will make him a great nation."

And God opened her eyes, and she saw a well of water. And she went and filled the skin with water, and gave the lad a drink.

Genesis 21:18,19 NKJV

God first told Hagar, "Arise." In order for her to help her son, she had to arise. She had to stand up before she could lift him.

Sometimes life's adversities against us put pressure on us to abort our dreams and visions. But though the vision tarries, you are to wait for it. It will come to pass.[9] If you are in lethargy, apathy, complacency, or fear, rise up from where you are!

As there was a well for Hagar, there is an oasis with your name on it. Only after Hagar rose up and lifted her son did God allow her eyes to be opened to see the oasis. Your provision is in your vision. Your resources are within reach. If you have asked Jesus to live inside you, you have everything you need. You just need to arise.

Even when all your natural resources have disappeared, rise up, find strength in God, who has it available for you, move on, and don't quit. Refuse to let your future die right before your very eyes.

El Roi Saw

The cry of the teenager made its way past the galaxy, through the celestial heavens, and right into the throne room of God. The cry of the son of Hagar commanded the attention of the God of the universe, the God she had so aptly named *El Roi*—the God who sees.

There at Beersheba, the "well of an oath,"[10] God reminded Hagar that nothing escapes His sight. Although she had taken her eyes off Him to see only the impeding obstacles on her journey, He had not taken His eyes off her and her son.

He had seen her begin to despair. Hagar could not sit idly by and watch her son gasp for his last breath, but she felt hopeless. Death was seemingly inevitable—until she heard the familiar voice of the Father of life.

He proved that He would not forsake the righteous. He refused to allow her to beg for bread. He knew exactly when the last drop of water and the last morsel of bread would be consumed. He was and is Jehovah-jireh, our Provider.[11] He was more than enough for Hagar and Ishmael, and He is more than enough for you and your offspring!

Sight Beyond What I See

Then God opened Hagar's eyes.

And God opened her eyes, and she saw a well of water. And she went and filled the skin with water, and gave the lad a drink.

Genesis 21:19 NKJV

Her pain and lack had blinded her view of the well that would revive her and her son and strengthen them to continue their journey. The invisible God had seen ahead and knew what was best for her and her son.

Your Well

I know as you read this chapter a dream inside you is about to be born. Everything within you senses change. My prayer for you is that during this season of change your eyes will be anointed to see the provision in your midst.

God will empower you to prosper. For Hagar, the well was always there, even when she didn't see it. Likewise, what you need is within your reach. Don't allow your marriage, your ministry, or your dream to die; there is a well within your midst.

Your well may be already with you. You may be walking past it day after day thinking it is your problem because you can't see what it contains. You may need to look beyond anything that is blocking your view and learn how to draw from the well that you already have.

The Well Inside You

As I draw from the well inside, I discover daily that I can do all things through Christ who strengthens me.[12] As a woman minister working in the Middle East, I heard everyone saying the ministry could not be effective. All the odds were stacked against me—a single, African-American mother! The odds kept stacking up, so I stopped counting them and started drawing from the well inside.

We were created to operate from the inside out. Paul said God separated him from his mother's womb and called him through His grace.[13] We can see through this example and also from the example of the prophet Jeremiah, whom God sanctified and ordained before Jeremiah was born,[14] that God predestines His plan for our lives.

Then He equips us with all that we need for the task, gives us the free will to submit to His will, and does an exceeding and abundant work in us *according to His power that is working within us,*[15] not according to external obstacles.

Every contradictory word spoken about my vision was only a human observation. My well that was springing up within me was a continual flow of confidence. My confidence was in knowing that He who had begun this work within me would be faithful to complete it even until the day of Jesus Christ.[16] He would watch over what He had placed inside of me to perform it.[17] He both wills and does of His good pleasure in me![18]

Now, years later, I train Arab men for leadership. By God's grace, they receive instruction from a woman. The anointing knows no gender! My anointing comes from my well within me. My well has supplied and enabled me to work in Saudi Arabia, Kuwait, Oman, Bahrain, and the United Arab Emirates. The favor that I walk in comes from the well I draw from.

Likewise, everything you need to accomplish all that He has ordained for you to do is inside of you. You need to let your well spring up within you today. Let that well make you whole, sharpen your vision, and enhance your calling. He who promised is faithful![19]

Strength To Finish the Journey

Once Hagar's eyes were opened, she drew water from the well of God's oath to her. The very covenant that she had received from God gave her the strength to finish her journey.

For Hagar and Ishmael, the life of the Lord's very presence annihilated the hand of death as did Jesus' death on the cross later, in the greatest magnitude, provide eternal life for all mankind. First Corinthians 15:54 says, "Death is swallowed up in victory." The victory was brought by Jesus' death on the cross and His resurrection. He came back to life, alive forevermore.[20] As *The Message* version of the Bible states, "...Death swallowed by triumphant Life!"[21] When life enters the scene, death must exit. Death has no sting, the grave no victory,[22] for those who have chosen to confess Jesus as Lord and believe that God raised Him from the dead.[23]

Not only did God sustain Ishmael's life on that seemingly hopeless day, but verse 20 tells us that God was with the lad as he grew. God kept His covenant promise to Hagar, who had been through so much rejection in life. No amount of pain or rejection was powerful enough to erase the promise Hagar clung to. As they journeyed in the wilderness, Ishmael grew and became a skillful archer.

So God was with the lad; and he grew and dwelt in the wilderness, and became an archer.

Genesis 21:20 NKJV

Hagar didn't take any chances when choosing her son's wife. To ensure that he would be accepted, she secured a wife for him from her own birth land, Egypt. Beginning with Ishmael, Hagar became the mother of all Arab peoples. The region they settled in was the region of Paran, modern-day Palestine.

God's plans are forever. Solomon tells us that whatever God does, nothing can be added, nor is anything powerful enough to take from it.[24] Everything He does is for eternity. The very best and the very worst of men cannot abort the Master's plan.

Although Isaac was the promised seed, God did not forsake His promise to Hagar. When Abraham forsook Ishmael, God did not forsake him. And He will not forsake Ishmael now. Many question how God will redeem the Arab Islamic nations. The answer is quite clear: The children of Ishmael who are operating outside of the Abrahamic covenant still long for the touch of their Father. Every morning the Islamic call to prayer is simply Ishmael crying out in the desert for the touch of his Father, and the only person who can reacquaint the Arab people with their Father is Jesus Christ.

Hagar received a covenant promise from God, and today Hagar's offspring can experience the benefits of that covenant. God's covenant with Abraham's seed does not position them above any other people on the face of the earth, although God will always honor His oath to Abraham. God is no respecter of persons, and because of Christ's redemption, the inheritance of God is available to everyone.

If God established a covenant with a woman who was a Gentile, a slave, a bond servant, how much more will He keep His covenant with you, His child whom He redeemed with His Son's own dear life? He is a covenant-keeping God. He is a faithful God. Not one of His promises will fail.

If He would visit a slave in the desert, then surely He longs to visit you right where you are at this very moment. Allow Him to work in you the inner beauty of submission, gentility, and quietness, for these together are a lethal force against the enemy. Let God carry every care. Cast your concerns upon Him. When you can't trace Him or track Him, trust Him. Trust His eyes to lead you and guide you every step of the way, and arise in trust that He will open your eyes to the promise that awaits you.

Prayer for the Attribute of Submission

Jesus, I know that the guidelines You have given us to follow are for our good, and with godly submission comes true liberation. Adhering to the godly attribute of submission is not easy to want to do. Everything within me feels taken advantage of as I am walking through this process. I know that you would never ask anything of me that You have not supplied to me first.

My flesh is screaming out to protect my free will to do things my own way! I can never mature my walk in the attribute of submission without Your help. I honestly don't understand why You would expect me to take the low road, the road less traveled, the road so few people want to take (but the one that you reward us for because in our humbling ourselves before you, you exalt us), time and time again, especially when those You require for me to submit to are walking contrary to Your counsel. It seems so unfair, Father, yet You know what is best for me; therefore, I call upon You now to help and strengthen me.

Help me hunger for humility in the midst of a society that protests for its right to rebel. When I am feeling that I am constantly being trodden underfoot, show me Your perfect plan for my life.

Help me see the peaceable fruit of righteousness that is being developed in me. Help me see how submission is my true liberation.

Father, I submit to You first before I can ever submit to man. You said that it is commendable to You when I endure patiently the persecution of doing good. In my heart I long to please You, and I thank You that You sent Jesus as my example. He suffered for my sake and opened not His mouth, but as I submit and commit to Him "who judges justly," I know that all things will work together for good for me—for those who love God and are called according to His purpose. I won't begin to pretend that this is easy, Father, because You already know my thoughts from afar. I know that You are in covenant with me. As I walk through this process of submission, I know that You have promised to never leave nor forsake me.

As I die daily to the dictates of my own self-will, rights, and opinions, I decrease so that You can increase in my life. My hope and joy lie within Your promise to me that is well pleasing to You as I submit to Your ordinances and counsel. I forfeit my way of doing things for Your divine blueprint for my life. I will not revolt against Your guidelines, because they have been orchestrated for my good. The strongest person is asked to take the road of submission. You saw that I, a woman, would have the ability to conform to the counsel of Your will at any cost. Thank You for seeing in me what I could never see in myself.

When my flesh desires to rebel and derail me from my purpose in You, help me submit to the leading of Your Holy Spirit. In my times of weakness, meet me and help me keep my tongue from reacting with evil words. Help me remember continually that I submit to

You because it is Your counsel for my life. You know my sitting down and my rising up. You know my strengths and my weaknesses and my end from my beginning. My confidence is in You, the master potter of my soul. Craft me, mold me, make me. Place me on Your wheel again and again until I am fully conformed to the counsel of Your will. Keep me in the furnace of Your purging fire until my character is a true reflection of Your nature. May I exemplify Your image and likeness to other women who are seeking identity.

Scriptures

Hebrews 12:11; 1 Peter 2:20-22 NIV; Isaiah 53:6,7,9-12; 1 Peter 2:23 NIV; Romans 8:28; Hebrews 13:5; 1 Corinthians 15:31; John 3:30; Psalm 139:2; Proverbs 3:23; Isaiah 29:16.

Daily Declaration

I decree by faith that I am decreasing daily and increasing in the wisdom and knowledge of the Almighty. When my heart is overwhelmed, I run to the Rock who is higher than I. I run to the Word and declare Your Word over the areas of my life that I have yet to submit to You. I understand now that submission is the highest form of trust. I choose to believe that I will never end up forsaken or abused because You are the God of my salvation and You cover and protect me from evil. You will not allow me to be consumed by evil men. I submit daily to You. I resist the devil who has to flee according to Your Word.

I will not respond to those who make mockery of my choice of submission. In due season You will exalt me in Your own way.

When I know that I am right in a situation, I choose to trust in Your requirement of submission. I forfeit my need to be first, right, and the best. I refuse to have the final say. As I submit, my soft tongue will continually turn away all wrath. Daily I look to You, Almighty, to give You my best.

PART 2

HANNAH: "LET'S MAKE A DEAL"

4

GOD WILL PREPARE YOUR WAY

Hannah stepped out of the box of tradition and "made a deal" with God. Her story begins during a time of great oppression in Israel. Pressure was mounting on every side as the Philistines, like an unfeeling bully, tormented the Israelites.

At that time, not only was the army of Israel weak, but the leadership of Israel was also in spiritual atrophy. The people still practiced the rituals of worship, but the spiritual corruption among God's appointed leaders caused His power and revelation to rarely manifest. Israel's rebellious state compromised their continual heavenly protection.

In the realm of the spirit, a major transition in the leadership was about to take place. It's likely safe to assume that a major reason Israel had once again returned to folly was that the spiritual leadership was not in order. Rather than be ruled by God alone, Israel wanted to be ruled by a human king and was about to shift their leadership from judges to kings. The anointing and focus of the two types of leadership were totally different.

Rule by opinion of the monarchial government was not the perfect will of God for Israel. God knew that the lifestyle of a king was far different from that of a priest or prophet. With access to lavish living, harems of women, power over people, and the ability to dictate his own agenda, a king would be less likely to live a life of consecration. Politics would come into play, as well as negotiations with pagan nations. This simply was not God's master design for His people.

However, just as a spoiled child whines to his parent to have his own way, so Israel did to God. The Israelites had lost their perspective of what God had created them to be and were willing to compromise their position as God's elect in order to fit in with their surrounding neighbors. It wasn't enough that their heavenly King had supernaturally provided for them in the wilderness.[1] Neither were they satisfied with His protection from the scorching desert sun or the chilling night winds and His provision through the pillar of cloud by day, with which He also led them, and the pillar of fire by night, by which He also provided light.[2] They had what other nations longed for, but they were willing to lay it all down to have what their surrounding nations had.

God created us *in His image*.[3] If we covet what others have, instead of celebrating what God has given us and who He has made us to be, day after day we will struggle to conform to an image of someone else and something less than the utmost He has planned for our lives. A lack of understanding of personal identity and purpose will blind our eyes to God's provision and protection, as well. When our vision is obscured and clouded, we fail to see the Most High as our source and resource in life.

Even though God warned the Israelites of what a king would do to them and their children, they persisted: "We want a king!" Finally, God gave them over to their own covetous desires. A king they wanted; a king they were about to receive.

A Spiritual Leader for Israel

This switch of genre in leadership was the beginning of a new era for Israel but not God's best. Israel badly needed spiritual renewal with strong leadership to bring prophetic insight and guidance. In this critical time of transition when God would take Israel from the rule of judges to that of kings, He needed a voice. He needed a servant who would be dedicated to Him and Him alone whom He knew would speak exactly as He commanded. He needed a servant who would speak His unaltered Word to kings and come to Him on behalf of His people, as well as fulfilling the priestly role of mediator.

God needs absolutely nothing outside Himself to exist. He is always more than enough and cannot be anything else because His nature, what flows out of Him, is to be more than enough. God—who is completely sufficient, never shortsighted, never caught off guard or empty-handed, never depleted or exhausted, the One who is the Way-maker—had a need. In fulfilling His sovereign plan for the work of His people, He needed a servant who would be unwilling to compromise or bow to the kingdoms and systems of man at a time when Israel was unaccustomed to hearing from God and unreceptive to following His direction. God needed a servant willing to live a consecrated life who would continue to hunger after Him with a heart that would remain sure to discerning and comprehending His ways, a seer who would discern by the spirit, not according to the flesh, to fulfill the role of the last judge and first prophet.

To have this kind of servant, God needed a life dedicated to Him from the origin, a child set apart for service to Him who would grow up undefiled by the influences of the former leadership even as he was being raised in its hands.

In this sense, God had a need. Also, through a barren woman who had a need, God would prepare the way for the new era of kings to begin. A great judge and prophet was about to be born. God, "I AM," eternity future and eternity past, omniscient, who knew Israel's present and future state, would cause this man to be born in the right time, nurtured in the right season, conceived by the right parents, and trained by the right leader.

The beauty of our God is His ability to always go ahead of us to prepare the way. Our heavenly Father looked down into the tunnel of time and marked Israel's dilemma. Then He petitioned a certain man and positioned him to begin preparing the way for the servant God needed to speak to Israel at this time. This man was Elkanah of Ramathaim Zophim (or "Ramah").[4]

Elkanah

Elkanah was living in the time before Israel had a king when every man in Israel did what was right in his own eyes.[5] Elkanah was a good man whose name one source defines as "the zeal of God,"[6] but he had fallen privy to the law of acceptance. You know that law we all have to contend with as believers: "Everybody else is doing it!" The original Law forbade polygamy, but in following the law of acceptance, Elkanah had two wives, Hannah and Peninnah. As we shall see, this arrangement would contribute to the Lord's plan.

This good man, Elkanah, had heard the rumors of the disorder in the sanctuary, no doubt. Although he was a Levite, he couldn't personally offer a sacrifice. This office was preserved for the priesthood. Elkanah knew he would have to submit his sacrificial offering to a fallen priest, but somehow had moved past setting his eyes on the priest to setting them on the Lord. Elkanah, who knew that God's command was for mankind to follow His ordinances, must have also settled within himself that they were God's route to salvation for His people.

Apparently, Elkanah must have drawn some conclusions to act upon. He must have received the revelation that God's power was not in the people who were administering the sacrifices, but ultimate grace was upon their lives to perform a particular duty and calling. There was a difference between the man and the office he filled—the man should not be esteemed higher than his office.

Never has there ever been a more accurate revelation to minister regarding all those in service of the king. We are who we are solely because of the grace of God, and by His grace He sovereignly communicates His will and message through us.

God has placed the excellency of His power in earthen vessels.[7] Some of these vessels are cracked and marked and some of them are ever leaking, yet they are still the Most High's vessels. In all of our frailties, God is longsuffering and patient. He is forever at work within us "…both to will and to do of his good pleasure."

Elkanah took his faith beyond the man and focused on his God. As in the temple,[8] he had to have some trust that this priest would go to God on behalf of him and his family.

We begin reading the details of the biblical account of God preparing the way for the servant through Elkanah in 1 Samuel 1. In verse 2, Hannah is mentioned as the first of Elkanah's two wives, and Peninnah as "the other." It is probable, then, that Hannah was his first wife; however, she was barren. Peninnah was a fertile mother of children. This could be an indication that Elkanah had procured Peninnah in order to produce a male child to secure his name and lineage.

Hannah's Rival

As a result, Peninnah seemed to anchor her confidence in her fertility. But because of her own ability to produce children for Elkanah, Peninnah demonstrated an insolent attitude toward Hannah. The women's relationship was so strained that the Bible actually calls Peninnah Hanna's rival:

> *Her rival also provoked her severely, to make her miserable, because the LORD had closed her womb.*

1 Samuel 1:6

Each time Peninnah became pregnant, Hannah remembered her own inadequacy. Time began wearing on her faith. With each passing season, she held on to her desire to bear a son, but her barrenness continued to weigh painfully on her soul.

So it was, year-by-year, when [Hannah] went up to the house of the LORD, that [Peninnah] provoked her; therefore she wept and did not eat.

1 Samuel 1:7

During the season of barrenness in Hannah's life, she was desperate and willing to do anything to receive the blessing of a child. Day in and day out, her need was right before her eyes. Everyone knew that she was barren. Her inadequacy was very visible. As she watched Peninnah at home with her children and other expectant women in the market, she passionately longed for the time that her reproach would be removed.

A Husband's Love

Hannah had come to a place where enough was enough! She was weary of Peninnah making a mockery of her situation. The rivalry between the two wives became increasingly intense, until it made Hannah miserable.

Then Elkanah her husband said to her, "Hannah, why do you weep? Why do you not eat? And why is your heart grieved? Am I not better to you than ten sons?"

1 Samuel 1:8

Her rival had not only sons but also daughters who easily wooed their way into their father's heart, but Elkanah loved Hannah, and her pain grieved him. Every year when the family went to Shiloh to worship, Elkanah gave Hannah a double portion for her offering, perhaps to make up for her void.[9]

Only God Could Meet the Need

Hannah's husband loved her and wanted to make things right for her, but the only One who could fulfill her deepest longing was God. He is also the Way-maker. He was preparing the way for the servant who would be His voice at this time in Israel's history just as, throughout the Old Testament times, He was preparing the way for the coming of The Way. God would send The Way, Jesus, The Servant, as God's voice, God's Word, to all humanity as the avenue to restore mankind's relationship with Him. In John 14:6 we read Jesus' statement: "I am the way, the truth, and the life. No one comes to the Father except through Me."

In order to be our divine navigator, He must step into our tomorrow. He must examine it, analyze it, secure it, prosper it, establish it, and validate it. Our future must meet His expectation, pass His inspection, and, most of all, be in cadence with His ultimate will.

With God, we live a fail-proof life. This is not an opposition-free life, but a fail-proof life. We see an example in the account of Joseph, beginning with Genesis 37:5, when God gave Joseph two dreams depicting a positive future. Little did Joseph know that the dreams represented the good outcome of evil events that he had not yet experienced. After Joseph lived through the events (described in Genesis chapters 37-50) initiated by the evil his brothers did to him, he experienced the positive outcome depicted in the dreams. Summarizing God's work to his brothers, Joseph said, "But as for you, you meant evil against me; but God meant it for good, in order to bring it about as it is this day, to save many people alive" (Gen. 50:20).

Through the example of the dreams, we see that God had stepped into Joseph's tomorrow and established and prospered it. In other words, what the enemy uses to oppose us and orchestrate for our failure, God has already inspected, validated, and destined for our good. He wants us to submit our will daily to His in order for Him to be able to do everything He wants to do for us and through us.

The Perfect Vessel

Hannah's barrenness not only depicted her own inadequacy, but also reflected Israel's spiritual state of being. God and Hannah had something in common as a point of meeting and negotiating. Hannah's infertility would be the very thing to make her the perfect vessel through which God could birth His plan, His servant totally dedicated to Him. During the season of her barrenness, she was desperate to do anything to please God. Because of her involvement, the events on earth would soon reflect His desire from heaven.

However, this was not the plight of Hannah. She had a need that demanded a supernatural seed, and God needed a yielded vessel. Hannah was willing to pay any price to have the blessing of a child. God needed someone who believed that all things were possible with Him.[10] In the midst of her inability, Hannah believed God's ability could enliven her womb.

In the design of the Most High, the weak display His strength, the simple show forth His wisdom, and the rejected are His elect. As Hannah walked in confidence that God held her life in His hands, her disappointments were about to be transformed into divine appointments, her stumbling blocks into stepping stones, the weapons of the enemy into tools in her hand to defeat the enemy.

Shiloh, the Place of Sacrifice

Willing to give God everything, Hannah decided that the ultimate place to offer a real sacrifice would be Shiloh. There, she would make a deal with God. Surely, she had given a lot of thought to her proposed offer. The annual journey from her home in Ramah to the tabernacle in Shiloh had provided all the time needed to weigh her decision.

As Hannah sought the author of life, Jehovah met the level of her increased expectancy, and Hannah reached out and touched the heart and hand of God.

> *Hannah arose after they had finished eating and drinking in Shiloh. Now Eli the priest was sitting on the seat by the doorpost of the tabernacle of the LORD. And she was in bitterness of soul, and prayed to the LORD and wept in anguish.*
>
> 1 Samuel 1:9,10 NKJV

Hannah cried out to the Lord. God had been endeavoring to work in Hannah's life and character all along to show her that her life was not about her ambitions or her dreams, but about fulfilling His plan for her, for her good, beyond any expectations she had for her destiny, and the good of others her destiny would affect.

Refuse Less Than God's Best

It's amazing the level of tolerance we have as females. Because we are adaptable creatures, we can easily conform to a substandard demand. When we get desperate enough for change, like Hannah, we will demand change.

We must refuse to settle for less than God's best for our lives.

God's eyes were upon Hannah for good. Maybe Hannah changed the way she normally prayed. She was persistent in refusing to let go of her desire. It was time to get what had been stolen from her. Her tears of reproach and shame were soon about to come to an end. Hannah transitioned past complaining to action.

She realized that if she continued to feel sorry for herself, then she would remain in the same position. Complaining can ensnare us and we must guard against it.[11] If we complain, we tend to continue to allow the thing we're complaining about to stay in our lives instead of doing something to change it. If we keep doing what we're doing, we'll keep getting what we're getting.

We are to present our bodies as a living sacrifice, holy, acceptable to God. We are also to present our minds, renewing them to God's Word to be transformed so that we may prove what is that good and acceptable and perfect will of God.[12] From reading and meditating on God's Word, we speak from the abundance of our heart in line with His Word,[13] and God watches over His Word to perform it.[14]

Purpose to abide in the Word of God, and allow the Word of God to abide in you. Then you can ask whatever you will and it will be done unto you.[15]

Our Father always hears us when we pray. As the Word of God germinates in you, it will build up your faith to the point that you believe anything is possible.[16]

As we mortify the deeds of our self-willed ambitions and crucify our intents, motives, and hidden agendas that are sometimes not openly apparent to us but are buried deeply within and rooted with guile, we will begin to see the fruit of righteousness in our lives. Only as we hide His Word in our hearts are we able to expose our secret desires that are contrary to His agenda so that we will fully cooperate as He works His plan out for us and with us.

Determine to live by this principle: Never complain about what you allow. Instead, decide to reposition yourself to receive God's best for you.

Determine and demand that things change in your life for the better. To get what you've never gotten, take a risk and do what you've never done.

Total Surrender

After Hannah reached this point of total surrender and prayed, she found she had moved into the very center of the perfect will of God. Stepping out of herself—her pains, her needs, and her ambitions—she walked directly into her divine purpose for the glory of God. Her life was not about her ambitions or her dreams, but about glorifying and honoring God alone.

When we come to the place of total surrender to Him, as Hannah did, God is able to do a work within us. Nothing we seek in life is truly about us. Everything that we accomplish and all that we are we owe to God.

5

A DIVINE EXCHANGE

The season of transitions had now come for Hannah, and she was now positioned in God to make a deal with Him. The prophet Isaiah tells us to reason together, and the sins of scarlet will be exchanged for purity as white as the driven snow.[1]

A divine exchange was about to take place between Hannah and God. Hannah carefully observed the needs at hand. She truly had a need. Her need was obvious; everyone knew her need. However, she was not the only one who had an open and exposed need. God also had a need. As did Elkanah, Hannah knew the state of Israel. The tabernacle was out of order. First Samuel 1:3 reveals that Hophni and Phinehas, the sons of Eli, were there at Shiloh. Not only were they there, but 1 Samuel 2 tells us that they were corrupt, taking advantage of the sacrifices (vv. 13-17) and "[lying] with the women who assembled at the door of the tabernacle of meeting" (v. 22 NKJV).

Living their whole lives with their father, Eli, the priest, the two men still "did not know the LORD" (1 Sam. 2:12). With all the prophetic insight that Eli had, he did not see and face the iniquity in his own household, and his compromise was about to cost him more than he bargained for.

Hannah's Prayer

At the same time, Hannah's prayer was about to afford her the greatest blessing of her life. Her promise was only days away, and God now had a willing vessel to trust Him wholeheartedly. Not leaning to her own understanding, in everything she acknowledged Him, and He was about to direct her path of destiny.

In the place of Hannah's brokenness, God was about to give her a son. In the place of God's need, Hannah was about to give Him a prophet. The Scriptures do not specify how long she had gone barren or how long her rival had mocked her, but we do know that Hannah was fed up with her situation. Something rose up within her that said, "I can't take it anymore! There must be a break-through for me."

Hannah refused to let go of her desire. The years of mockery and reproach had taken their toll on her, and she had reached her point of no return. It was time to get what had been stolen from her. Her tears of reproach and shame would soon come to an end. God's eyes were upon Hannah for good.

A New Motive

In the beginning stages, all Hannah desired was for her reproach and shame to be removed. Her motive of prayer had been completely self-motivated, but her daily visitations into the throne

A DIVINE EXCHANGE

room of His presence had caused her to decrease and Him to increase in her life.[2]

Slowly, as Hannah had waited on God for the blessing of a child, her selfish ambition had decreased and her will had begun to bow to the will of the Father. When she entered the tabernacle at Shiloh this time, it was no longer about what she wanted, but rather what she could give the Lord.

Through intimate fellowship, Hannah had learned the ways of her Master. She had learned how to please Him, how to minister to Him, how to love Him, and how to sacrifice to Him. Hannah saw her Lord's need, and her Lord saw her need. Both needed a son.

Finally, as she yielded to her Master's will, Hannah made a serious vow unto the Lord.

Hannah's Vow

Hannah needed a son to remove her reproach, and God needed a son to remove His reproach. Eli's sons were a reproach to God before all of Israel. God needed an upright man of character and integrity. Seeing this, Hannah took the biggest risk of her life and made a promise that God could not refuse:

> Then she made a vow and said, "O LORD of hosts, if You will indeed look on the affliction of Your maidservant and remember me, and not forget Your maidservant, but [if You] will give Your maidservant a male child, then I will give him to the LORD all the days of his life, and no razor shall come upon his head."
>
> 1 Samuel 1:11 NKJV

69

Hannah offered the hope of a future son to God. If He would give her a son, then she would give her son back to God as a servant in the tabernacle.

Hannah's Risk

Hannah risked everything for God's purpose to be manifested in her life. Her vow would mean offering her son into the care of the priesthood for his entire life. She would forego her right and ability to raise her own child. She would miss the developmental stages of his life on a daily basis.

Hannah's vow would cost not only her, but her son. There would be no doubt concerning his role and purpose. He would be a Nazarite, a man separated for the Lord's service. He himself would have to make a special vow to live a life of total consecration to the Lord. No alcohol would touch his lips; no razor would come near his head, and he would never make contact with a dead body.[3] He would be completely devoted to the service of the Lord.

Consider the risk that Hannah would have to take to give her baby over to the service of the Lord in the tabernacle. The priest's household, in which her son would be reared, was highly dysfunctional. In his old age, Eli told his sons, "I hear of your evil dealings from all the people" (1 Sam. 2:23). Eli upbraided his sons for their wickedness, but they both refused to listen to his instructions. Their hearts were set on doing evil, and Eli could do nothing to change them. How could Hannah risk placing a child in the hands of this priest who was dull of hearing and lethargic toward his calling?

But Hannah's faith was not in the priest. Hannah's faith was in God. Hannah positioned herself before God and walked by faith, not by sight.[4] The only thing that mattered to her at that moment was making this divine exchange with the Maker of all life.

Hannah Made a Scene

While she met God at the altar and wept bitterly before Him, Hannah spoke out to the Lord all that was in her heart. Hannah's lips moved, but no one but God could hear her request. Her desire was too deep for words to articulate. Out of the abundance of her heart, her mouth spoke. Eli was standing in the door of the temple watching Hannah's actions. She didn't look and sound like the other women praying in a traditional manner. She was moved to a height of emotion that Eli had never witnessed before—so much so that he thought she was drunk.

> And it happened, as she continued praying before the Lord, that Eli watched her mouth. Now Hannah spoke in her heart; only her lips moved, but her voice was not heard. Therefore Eli thought she was drunk. So Eli said to her, "How long will you be drunk? Put your wine away from you!"
>
> 1 Samuel 1:12-14 NKJV

Nothing Caused Her To Stumble

Hannah could have easily become offended by Eli's accusation, but she didn't. The Word of God decrees, "Great peace have those who love Your law, and nothing causes them to stumble" (Ps. 119:165 NKJV).

Hannah was holding on to her hope in God. She had made a vow unto the Lord, a powerful covenant decree that couldn't be broken. The Bible says that it is better not to make a vow than to make one and not keep it.[5] Hannah would now have to risk placing her child in the hands of this man who now stood before her accusing her of being drunk, this man who was failing with his own children. But her confidence was not in the opinions or validations of man. Her confidence was in the Word of the Lord.

Always remember that your faith is between you and God. God always deals with you according to your own measure of faith.[6] No one can limit, ambush, or steal your faith. You determine how far you want to go in God. Be it unto you according to your faith.[7] Your faith will make you whole.[8]

Eli's opinion did not divert Hannah's focus. She harnessed her thoughts and disconnected herself from the opinions of men so that her instructions and directions were chartered from heaven.

She was willing to give up her first son—not to man, but to the only One who could give him to her. Knowing that she may never have another, she gave up her pride, her longing, her son.

Despite Eli's challenging accusation, Hannah responded with a gentle answer, which turns away anger.[9]

> *"...No, my lord, I am a woman of sorrowful spirit. I have drunk neither wine nor intoxicating drink, but have poured out my soul before the LORD. Do not consider your maidservant a wicked woman, for out of the abundance of my complaint and grief I have spoken until now."*

> 1 Samuel 1:15,16 NKJV

In one moment's time Hannah went from accusation to confirmation. The age-old priest feebly transitioned from his mistaken impression of intoxication to the most comforting words that Hannah could ever await. The Word of God tells us to believe His prophets and we will be established. The word the priest gave Hannah was all that she needed to boost her confidence and to maintain her posture of faith and patience. The aging priest spoke over Hannah and said, "God grant her...." This was Hannah's earnest desire spoken through the priest. At that moment she paralleled the demeanor of Mary, the mother of Jesus, "Be it unto me according to thy word" (Luke 1:38) and will.

"Go in Peace"

Hannah's desire to have a child would not change, but she would soon put her complaint and grief behind her.

> Then Eli answered and said, "Go in peace, and the God of Israel grant your petition which you have asked of Him."
>
> And she said, "Let your maidservant find favor in your sight." So the woman went her way and ate, and her face was no longer sad.
>
> 1 Samuel 1:17,18 NKJV

The word of the high priest was equivalent to a prophetic word, and Hannah believed that God would indeed grant her petition. Just as Hannah trusted God's Word, she counted on Him to trust hers. She expected to keep her word and trusted Him to keep His, regardless of the circumstances.

The vacuum in Hannah's life had lasted long enough to fill her heart with an earnest desire for a son, and she had fulfilled God's desire by making her vow: "If you open my womb, I'll give my son back to You to serve You all the days of his life."

God Opened Her Womb

Hannah had made her own covenant with God, and He honored her and opened her womb. What was once barren was now fertile.

> So it came to pass in the process of time that Hannah conceived and bore a son, and called his name Samuel, saying, "Because I have asked for him from the LORD."
>
> 1 Samuel 1:20 NKJV

Hannah's heart was full! Her greatest desire had been met. Her newborn son looked into her eyes as she nursed him. How beautiful he was to her. She had never known such love. But she knew this bond that had formed so quickly would soon be interrupted by the vow she had made. Her heart must have rebelled within her, wanting so badly to take her promise back; but she would never fail on her promise to the One who had fulfilled His promise to her. Hannah nursed her newborn son and continued to care for him until he was weaned. Hannah honored her word and made the biggest sacrifice of her life. She brought Samuel to the tabernacle to offer him, her only son, to the Lord, just as she had promised.

> Now when she had weaned him, she took him up with her, with three bulls, one ephah of flour, and a skin of wine, and brought him to the house of the LORD in Shiloh. And the child was young. Then they slaughtered a bull, and brought the child to Eli. And she said, "O my lord! As your soul lives, my lord, I am the woman who stood by you here, praying to the LORD. For this child I prayed, and the LORD has granted me my petition which I asked of Him.

> *Therefore I also have lent him to the LORD; as long as he lives he*
> *shall be lent to the LORD...."*
>
> 1 Samuel 1:24-28 NKJV

Hannah's heart must have swelled with emotion. How grateful she must have been to know that she was honoring God with everything she could possibly give. At the same time, how broken she must have felt as she walked away from everything her heart ever wanted.

Though she could only play a small part in Samuel's life from that day forward, she knew God had a plan for him.

> *But Samuel ministered before the Lord, even as a child, wearing a*
> *linen ephod. Moreover his mother used to make him a little robe,*
> *and bring it to him year by year when she came up with her*
> *husband to offer the yearly sacrifice.*
>
> 1 Samuel 1:18,19 NKJV

The focus most often is on Hannah's sacrificial willingness to offer her first and only born son. However, Elkanah had to also make a decision to offer his son to the Lord and into the hands of a disorderly priest!

Just imagine, God ordained a man to give His long-awaited son to a man, a *priest,* whose sons God said had "made themselves vile, and he [Eli] did not restrain them" (1 Sam. 3:13 NKJV). God had "...sworn to the house of Eli that the iniquity of Eli's house shall not be atoned for by sacrifice or offering forever" (1 Sam. 3:14 NKJV).

Because Eli knew of his sons' iniquity and had not restrained them, God swore and he did not restrain them. God's sovereign plan is not always the most obvious. It most commonly comes with major challenges that demand that the vessel trust Him alone.

Elkanah had already settled within himself to submit his sacrificial offerings to a fallen priest. He had seen that the man should not be esteemed higher than his office.

As we look into the life of Elkanah, we can see that his preparation didn't begin only on his annual journey to Shiloh, which was coincidentally the only place on earth that there was a sanctuary at that time. As a tither, Elkanah had to learn to trust God with his resources and minister to the Lord his rightful portion. As a tither, he had to offer at least three solemn feasts. You see, Elkanah would go with his father during the Passover feasts and other annual times of feasts during that time. As a Levite and a man from a region interpreted "watchman," he had to trust the supreme watchman to watch over his son.

God Filled Hannah's Arms

Hannah continued to be in Samuel's life as much as she could, but her arms ached to hold her own child. God saw Hannah's longing, as did Eli the priest.

> And Eli would bless Elkanah and his wife, and say, "The LORD give you descendants from this woman for the loan that was given to the LORD." Then they would go to their own home.
>
> 1 Samuel 2:20 NKJV

In response to the longing of His faithful servant's heart, God made Hannah a mother, not of one child, but of many:

And the LORD visited Hannah, so that she conceived and bore three sons and two daughters. Meanwhile the child Samuel grew before the Lord.

1 Samuel 2:21 NKJV

Hannah's heart was full with the blessing of God. She had said, "Lord, let's make a deal," and because of it both Hannah and the Lord had met a need.

He Has Already Worked It Out

Long before Hannah was born, God saw into her life and knew that she would desire a son enough to offer him to His service. He saw her need, and His answer was awaiting her even before she was conceived.

I believe that through the pages in this book, God is confirming to you that He has already worked everything out for your good. I don't know what you are up against at this very moment, but God is more than able to go ahead of you and make every crooked path straight for you.[10] He has orchestrated every detail of this journey on your behalf. No plot of the enemy is big enough to cancel God's agenda for your life. Nebuchanezzer couldn't go up against the Almighty; Pharaoh's stubborn will had to bow to His counsel. God's Word declares,

The counsel of the LORD stands forever, the plans of His heart to all generations.... The LORD looks from heaven; he sees all the sons of men.... He fashions their hearts individually; he considers all their works.

Psalm 33:11,13,15 NKJV

The plans of God's heart are eternal.

Everything that is before you now is visible to God—every concern, every question. In the unfolding of God's plan, every single detail is significant. He shall direct and establish your path.[11] He has already ordered your steps.[12] The way of the Lord is sure concerning you.

God is always a step ahead of the enemy. The Bible says the Lamb [Jesus] was slain before the foundations of the world.[13] Before the enemy ever conceives, entertains, or plots his ambushes, even his craftiest schemes, God knows them. They are all naked and exposed before Him.

God always goes ahead of His people to clear their path, and He specifically prepares every detail. He leaves no stone left unturned, no intricate detail overlooked. His way is perfect.

He worked His perfect plan through Hannah, and her sacrifice made it possible. In Samuel, Hannah had a son and her reproach was forever removed. And in Samuel, God had a man through whom He would speak to the nation of Israel and anoint the first king in the nation, David, from whose line would come the King of kings, who would remove all reproach for all eternity.

Prayer for Waiting on the Lord

Lord, help me to be patient when everything within my soul wants to take matters into my own hands. Help me to be still and command my heart, mind, and body to yield and conform totally to Your way of doing things. Lord, please let there be nothing within me that revolts against Your will.

Father, while I am waiting, help me to be still and find joy and peace in my state of waiting. Help me to focus not only on the fulfillment of my desire, but give me an insatiable appetite to see Your full work completed within me. Lord, please continue to remind me during this process of waiting that my character is being changed. Continue to remind me that my waiting is not in vain. You said that strength comes to those who wait upon the Lord.

Lord, please strengthen me so that I may never give up or give in during my season of waiting. Make me persistent and give me Holy Ghost stamina to endure until the end. When I feel myself about to faint I will call upon You, Lord, to answer me in my weakest hour and meet me with Your divine fortitude. In Your presence, Oh Lord, I find the peace and stamina I need for my challenges. Remind me that as each day comes to a close, I am closer and closer to my promise. Help me to take one day at a time and find Your lesson to me in each given day. Every morning that I arise, let's make a covenant with each other to be in constant communion and fellowship. You not only want me to obtain the promise, but to learn my life's lessons during the process of waiting.

I bind anxiety that comes to torment my mind. I know that You will never forget or forsake me. I forget sometimes that the Holy Spirit is my teacher during this season of my life. He is also my comfort during the journey. Fear will have no hold over me because I have chosen to walk in the love of God. Once I have endured, I will be able to strengthen my fellow man. This helps me to understand more and more that what I am enduring is not only about me, but this is equipping me to be a help to others. Thank You, Lord, that You know the set and appointed time. You are never in a rush because You are eternal, Oh Lord, and You know I am a human bound by time. You have given me an advocate, Christ Jesus my Lord and redeeming intercessor. He sits next to You and He knows Your most intimate desires for me. I thank You, Father, that He ever lives to make intercession for me in the midst of my waiting.

Scriptures

Psalm 25:3; Psalm 69:6; Lamentations 3:25; 1 Kings 17:16.

Daily Declaration

Today I choose to allow patience to have its perfect work in me so that when the work is finished I will be made whole and complete. I will be able to live a life free from lack. I declare that I am a woman or man of patience. I possess everlasting endurance, divine stamina, and fervent fortitude to endure any challenge that comes to oppose and impede upon my undisturbed composure.

I mount up as an eagle as I wait upon the Lord. I will never be put to shame because I am waiting on my Master. He is good to me because I wait upon Him. I am a blessed man or woman because I wait for the performance of my Savior. I am persistent and will not faint; I purpose to endure until the end until full manifestation of my expected anticipation becomes reality. My earnest hope is in the name of the Lord. I add to my faith perseverance and to perseverance, godliness. My present tribulation is producing perseverance in me, and my perseverance will produce character according to Romans 5:3.

There is no other way to obtain patience and godly character without perseverance and endurance. What seems to be a time of disappointment for me is actually my season of development for greater things that await me in my predestined future. So I rejoice, knowing that He who has begun a good work in me is completing it and is working everything within me after the council of His will. According to Hebrews 13:21, I am being made complete in every good work to do His will, and He is working in me what is pleasing in His sight through Jesus Christ.

PART 3

ABIGAIL:
MARRIED TO A FOOL

6

A WOMAN OF GREAT WISDOM

A mong the women risktaker role models whose strengths, weaknesses, victories, and failures the Bible displays as examples given us to follow, is a woman of great wisdom, Abigail. As Solomon said, there is nothing new under the sun.[1] He also gave us sobering insight that life repeats itself in seasons, times, dispensations, and cultures. "That which is now already has been, and that which is to be already has been; and God seeks that which has passed by [so that history repeats itself]" (Eccl. 3:15 AMP).

Humanity's fears, intimidating behaviors, ego-driven desires, character qualities, and questions about life unfold in different persons in different ways in different eras of time, but the needs of mankind remain the same. Both men and women want to be loved, respected, honored, appreciated, heard, and validated. Even the very strongest of human beings seek these components to life, fulfilling the needs of the woman in the man and the man in the woman.

Abigail's name means "father rejoices,"[2] and we will see how with her wisdom and courage she made her heavenly Father rejoice.

When we master what God has given us, we can easily find our path to celebrating our womanhood. We are indeed fearfully and wonderfully made.[3] God did such a work in us that after He had finished He rested, stepped back, and called it, including us, good.[4]

God's design for the woman was to complement the man[5]—to complete him in his strengths and weaknesses. This is a function that Abigail learned well to fulfill.

Married to a Fool

Abigail married Nabal, a wealthy rancher, whose dowry must have been very advantageous to her father and family. We do not know how he acquired his wealth. He could have inherited it, and the ranch could have been passed down from his family's previous generations. The Bible does not say. One thing we do know, though, is that his wealth did not make him a wise person.

Nabal means "fool," and his name adequately describes him. Nabal's foolish decisions and behavior were visible to the whole village. We do not know why Abigail married a fool. Perhaps their marriage had been arranged by their parents. Maybe she thought she could change him, as many women think they can change the men in their lives. But we do know that she learned to complete him, rather than trying to change him.

The Bible describes Abigail as a woman of good understanding and beautiful appearance. She was not a woman of glamour with no substance, but instead exemplified the teaching the apostle Peter would later write: "Do not let your adornment be merely outward...rather let it be the hidden person of the heart, with the incorruptible beauty of a gentle and quiet spirit, which is very precious in the sight of God" (1 Peter 3:3,4 NKJV).

While Abigail was notably wise, her husband, Nabal, was harsh and evil in his dealings. It was bad enough that his name meant "fool," but foolishness and evil are a bad combination. It was because of these poor qualities in Nabal's life that Abigail would meet Israel's future King David.

The Journey of the Future King

David's meeting with Abigail occurred at a pivotal time in his life. The prophet Samuel, who had anointed him as the future king,[6] had recently died,[7] and David's present surroundings seemed diabolically opposed to everything that Samuel had prophesied of him.

Shortly after being anointed as the future king, David received an invitation from King Saul to play the harp to soothe his demonically tormented soul.[8] David later served the king in battle, killing not only the giant Goliath but many Philistines.[9] As the people praised David for his valor, though, in a sudden fit of jealousy, Saul sought David's death.[10]

David fled from Saul, and the king and three thousand men pursued him. In a divine sequence of events, Saul arrived in the very cave in which David hid. While there, David quietly cut off a piece of Saul's robe.[11]

However, feeling convicted, David repented before God and King Saul for his sly behavior. Humbly, David said, "'Wickedness proceeds from the wicked.' But my hand shall not be against you" (1 Sam. 24:13 NKJV). Once Saul had seen his cut robe and David holding the torn government in his hand, he realized that David could have taken his life. Saul's heart was convicted as he realized David had spared his life, and he went home.[12]

David's Act of Submission

By seeking Saul's forgiveness, David had displayed submission to the king, which 1 Peter 2:13-14 NIV addresses:

> *"Submit yourselves for the Lord's sake to every authority instituted among men: whether to the king, as the supreme authority, or to governors, who are sent by him to punish those who do wrong and to commend those who do right."*

Regardless of Saul's actions and motives, David harnessed his will and emotions and subjected them to the commitment of his character. David's strength of character not only helped him submit to the king, but even kept him from killing him when it seemed that "God delivered [him] into [his] hand" (1 Sam. 24:4,9,18).

Shortly after this courageous exhibit of honor and character, though, David soon found himself being tested by his very own words. David had shown so much kindness to one who had responded with much evil. Now once again he would show kindness to one who would arise to reject him.

David's Request

Soon after King Saul's surrender and departure, David and his men camped in a particular village named Maon. Nabal lived in this village but was away shearing his sheep in Carmel. When David and his men needed sustenance, David could have easily ordered his men to simply take some of the herd and have a great feast. But he refused to operate that way and would not allow his men or anyone else to take Nabal's possessions as he was away on business.

However, on a feast day, David sent ten of his men to greet Nabal in peace on his behalf and to request that Nabal consider compensating them for taking care of his possessions. David knew Nabal was a prosperous man and would not miss anything that was given to David and his men because food was so plenteous, especially at the time of the feast.

Nabal's Refusal

Without a thought, though, Nabal flatly refused David's request.

Then Nabal answered David's servants, and said, "Who is David, and who is the son of Jesse? There are many servants nowadays who break away each one from his master. Shall I then take my bread and my water and my meat that I have killed for my shearers, and give it to men when I do not know where they are from?"

1 Samuel 25:10,11 NKJV

Nabal may have been unaware that David was widely renowned for his valor in battle (and was capable of bringing him great harm) and that David was God's choice as the future king of Israel. Or he may have been lying when he said he didn't know of David and his men.

Solomon sums up the way of a fool in Proverbs 14:8 that the folly of fools is always deceit. Whether Nabal knew who had requested the food or not, keeping his wealth to himself was more important than David or anyone else.

Blinded by Greed

Blinded by greed, Nabal was in direct violation of a command found in Nehemiah 8:10 NKJV: "Go your way, eat the fat, drink the sweet, and send portions to those for whom nothing is prepared...." God never takes offense to our wealth, but He gives us very clear instructions for handling that wealth. Everything we possess belongs to God alone, and He wants us to be His distribution vessels for those in need.

Nabal was foolish enough to think that he was the proprietor of his total wealth. He did not understand that to assist David would be to bless the Lord. When we minister to the needs of man, we give unto our Master.

The Bible says that Nabal was a descendent of Caleb. His predecessors had lived in a household that had experienced God's miraculous outpouring of divine provision and protection. If any man should have been appreciative of the goodness of God and willing to give something back, it was Nabal.

But Nabal was a fool. A fool is right in his own eyes and doesn't seek intelligent counsel. (Prov. 12:15.) Nabal was married to a woman of understanding, yet he did not even seek her wisdom. Proverbs 1:7 tells us that fools despise wisdom and instruction. What Nabal needed to be completed and made whole was right within his own household: Her name was Abigail. She had everything he needed to absolve him of his foolishness, if only he would have asked.

Stirred to Action

When the ten servants told David what Nabal had said, David was furious. The words of a fool arouse strife.[13] Nabal's refusal stirred David's anger because he had questioned the integrity of his character: "Who is David, and who is the son of Jesse? There are many servants nowadays who break away each one from his master" (1 Sam. 25:10,11 NKJV). David felt the stab of Nabal's words questioning his loyalty, when no one had been more loyal toward King Saul than he.

"Who is David? Who is David?" Nabal's words must have rung in his ears. "I will show you who David is." And his anger was stirred to action.

> Then David said to his men, "Every man gird on his sword." So every man girded on his sword, and David also girded on his sword. And about four hundred men went with David, and two hundred stayed with the supplies.
>
> 1 Samuel 25:13 NKJV

In his rage, David ordered his four hundred men to grab their swords. He had fire in his eyes, and his target was not only Nabal but also every male on the premises.

The Shearers Seek Abigail's Counsel

The shearers couldn't believe their ears! Frustrated at their master Nabal, they must have thought, *You really are a fool! Your folly and loose words are going to kill all of us!*

One young man among them eased away and told Abigail the situation. It was as if he knew that the only hope for their lives would be found in the mouth of Abigail. During this time in history, the advice and opinions of women were not typically highly esteemed, but Abigail had the trust of her people and was known as a woman of great understanding. She had obviously displayed character and wisdom before, because the young man ran straight to her for a remedy.

> Now one of the young men told Abigail, Nabal's wife, saying, "Look, David sent messengers from the wilderness to greet our master; and he reviled them. But the men were very good to us, and we were not hurt, nor did we miss anything as long as we accompanied them, when we were in the fields. They were a wall to us both by night and day, all the time we were with them keeping the sheep. Now therefore, know and consider what you will do, for harm is determined against our master and against all his household. For he is such a scoundrel that one cannot speak to him."
>
> 1 Samuel 25:14-17 NKJV

Terrified at the possibility of David acting on his words, the herdsmen were desperate to receive sound counsel from Abigail. And they would soon discover that she was a good source for help. Unlike her husband, she was quick to consider the welfare of her people. Quickly, she executed her own plan.

7

ABIGAIL'S PLAN

A bigail moved expeditiously to spare the men whose lives were now placed in her care.

Then Abigail made haste and took two hundred loaves of bread, two skins of wine, five sheep already dressed, five seahs of roasted grain, one hundred clusters of raisins, and two hundred cakes of figs, and loaded them on donkeys. And she said to her servants, "Go on before me; see, I am coming after you." But she did not tell her husband Nabal.

1 Samuel 25:18,19 NKJV

As a matriarchal intercessor, Abigail prepared a meal for all of David's men. Thankfully, she had built her house and her community wisely and had her servants' trust and favor, so they listened to her and helped her.

Abigail had to orchestrate a strategy that would cover the height and breadth of her husband's foolishness. Therefore, she had to think through everything thoroughly. Providing the food was a small component to the remedy. She also had to build a case to appeal to David's heart in order to reverse his decree against Nabal. Knowing that she was opposing her own husband's will, Abigail prepared to go before the future king of Israel to plead the case of her people.

Abigail's Journey

Quickly Abigail headed toward the man who would decide their fate.

> So it was, as she rode on the donkey, that she went down under cover of the hill; and there were David and his men, coming down toward her, and she met them. Now David had said, "Surely in vain I have protected all that this fellow has in the wilderness, so that nothing was missed of all that belongs to him. And he has repaid me evil for good. May God do so, and more also, to the enemies of David, if I leave one male of all who belong to him by morning light."
>
> 1 Samuel 25:20-22 NKJV

Time was running out. Abigail had to speak quickly and accurately to dismantle the weapons aimed at her doorstep. Approaching David, she must have prayed for wisdom and fluent speech.

Surely this was not the first predicament Abigail had gotten Nabal out of. Through the years of their marriage, she had learned to rely on intense words of wisdom. In this present situation, each word would have to reveal her wisdom and understanding to David.

Meeting With the Future King

Reaching the place where David and his men stood prepared to attack, Abigail humbly bowed and made her case before her future king.

Now when Abigail saw David, she dismounted quickly from the donkey, fell on her face before David, and bowed down to the ground. So she fell at his feet and said: "On me, my lord, on me let this iniquity be! And please let your maidservant speak in your ears, and hear the words of your maidservant.

"Please, let not my lord regard this scoundrel Nabal. For as his name is, so is he: Nabal is his name, and folly is with him! But I, your maidservant, did not see the young men of my lord whom you sent. Now therefore, my lord, as the LORD lives and as your soul lives, since the LORD has held you back from coming to bloodshed and from avenging yourself with your own hand, now then, let your enemies and those who seek harm for my lord be as Nabal."

1 Samuel 25:23-25 NKJV

This wise woman used her skill and carefully selected her words to convey a different point of view to David, who stood before her as a bloodthirsty warrior. Abigail's intelligence and understanding were as acute as a defense attorney's during a murder trial. Line upon line, she pled the case of her household before David. Knowing the outcome could have been her own death, she risked her life to save countless others.

Abigail demonstrated the role of a true Proverbs 31 woman:

She opens her mouth with wisdom, and on her tongue is the law of kindness. She watches over the ways of her household....

Proverbs 31:26,27 NIV

Conceding the ignorance of her husband and his acts of iniquity, Abigail acknowledged that David was justified in his request and had every right to be compensated.

Abigail's Gift

Moreover, Abigail put works to her faith and trusted that she would find favor in David's sight. The Bible tells us that faith without works is dead.[1] Not depending on her words alone, Abigail brought something tangible to demonstrate her intent, saying,

> *"And now this present which your maidservant has brought to my lord, let it be given to the young men who follow my lord."*
>
> 1 Samuel 25:27 NKJV

Abigail could see the change in David's eyes as she took the position of humility and used not only humble words but the gift of food to convey her appeal.

Abigail Praised David's Character

With a deep breath, Abigail prepared herself to deliver the intent of her message. She knew that her selection of words would have to derail her audience from the track of anger and revenge that they had been vehemently going down. With her head bowed, she spoke:

> *"Please forgive the trespass of your maidservant. For the LORD will certainly make for my lord an enduring house, because my lord fights the battles of the LORD, and evil is not found in you throughout your days."*
>
> 1 Samuel 25:28 NKJV

Abigail took upon herself all of the weight of responsibility for her foolish husband's behavior. At the same time, she praised David. Every man on the face of the earth likes to hear someone speak well of his character. Abigail reminded David of his righteous character.

Abigail Understood

Then, showing her understanding of David's predicament, she carefully shifted the focus of her speech to the problem of King Saul:

> *"Yet a man has risen to pursue you and seek your life, but the life of my lord shall be bound in the bundle of the living with the LORD your God; and the lives of your enemies He shall sling out, as from the pocket of a sling."*

1 Samuel 25:29 NKJV

David was favored in the eyes of the people, and everyone knew how insane King Saul had become in his pursuit of David. Seeing how this had negatively affected David's judgment, narrowing his view to only see the moment, Abigail wisely pointed him back toward his future.

> *"And it shall come to pass, when the LORD has done for my lord according to all the good that He has spoken concerning you, and has appointed you ruler over Israel, that this will be no grief to you, nor offense of heart to my lord, either that you have shed blood without cause, or that my lord has avenged himself. But when the LORD has dealt well with my lord, then remember your maidservant."*

1 Samuel 25:30,31 NKJV

Abigail's speech reminded him of the strong character traits that he possessed: the most important being self-restraint, which he had shown to a great degree when he'd let Saul, his pursuer, go in peace. Then Abigail caused David to see that his decision to attack Nabal and his people was contrary to the reputation of his character.

Left unchecked, he would kill Nabal and all the men on Nabal's land, forever marring his reputation among the people of Israel.

A Voice for God

Abigail's words were persuasive, and her motives were unselfish. She was operating as a voice of God interceding for the lives of her people. Abigail had to trust that God would empower her with each word of wisdom that she needed. *If anyone knows the heart of David, it is God,* she thought. So she depended not upon her alluring ways as a woman, but on the counsel of the Lord.

David himself wrote that the counsel of the Lord is what will always stand forever.[2] As women, when we are facing seemingly impossible situations, especially ones that involve our husbands, children, bosses, colleagues, or relatives, we must depend upon God alone to change those situations. When we lack wisdom, we need to go directly to the source of all wisdom. God has granted us this very special promise in James 1:5 (NKJV):

> *If any of you lacks wisdom, let him ask of God, who gives to all liberally and without reproach, and it will be given to him.*

God will not hold back any amount of wisdom from us, if we ask. To be wise, like Abigail, all we have to do is ask.

A Soft Tongue Turned Away Wrath

Abigail operated in the most incredible wisdom toward David. She reminded him that his calling was to fight the battles of the

Lord. Clearly, this battle against Nabal was not the Lord's battle but David's own personal battle to vindicate his bruised ego.

The Law plainly stated that murder for a personal agenda was wrong. Nabal had not physically injured David; he had simply refused to grant him his request. David had been humiliated and insulted before his men and had decided to kill innocent people without taking the time to make a moral judgment of the situation.

Proverbs 16:18 says that pride goes before a fall. We must not take credit for our victories but give the glory to God. We are who we are by the grace of God, and that is all we will ever be. As we remain grateful to God and small in our own eyes, we will avoid the mess that David almost caused himself when he allowed pride to cloud his judgment.

Yes, the Lord had backed David as he had killed in war and in defense. But in this situation David was just angry at Nabal for his ignorance, and he was about to make everyone else suffer for it. Everyone knew that Nabal was the village idiot, but David's planned response would not have been a judicious execution or an impersonal act of warfare. It would have been sinful retaliation.

Abigail, and even David, knew that this was clearly a case of revenge. David had decided to take matters into his own hands instead of calling on the name of the Lord to avenge him.

David Had Forgotten His Own Words

Seemingly suffering from momentary amnesia, David forgot the words he himself had written: "Let all those rejoice who put their trust in You...because You defend them. For You, O LORD, will bless the righteous; with favor You will surround him as with a shield" (Ps. 5:11,12 NKJV).

He had forgotten the sound instructions he had written when Saul had pursued him: "It is God who avenges me, and subdues the peoples under me; He delivers me from my enemies. You also lift me up above those who rise against me; You have delivered me from the violent man" (Ps. 18:47,48 NKJV).

Abigail's words of wisdom reminded David of his own experiences and the wisdom he had gained in his intimate moments with God. The words of this wise woman pointed David back to the Law of the Lord and into the direction of his calling. Abigail's soft answer defused David's wrath[3] and navigated him back to purpose.

Focused on Purpose

This is exactly what a wise person does: She keeps her compass dial on purpose. Abigail's purpose at that moment was not to save herself but her husband. Whether he realized it or not, Nabal needed her. And she stepped into her purpose when she intervened in order to cover Nabal's weaknesses, which could have brought his whole village into calamity.

Abigail pointed David back to the Law of the Lord, and he knew that Law was perfect. He himself had written, "As for God, His way is perfect; the word of the LORD is proven; He is a shield to all who trust in Him" (Ps. 18:30 NKJV). He had once prayed, "Your word I have hidden in my heart, that I might not sin against You" (Ps. 119:11 NKJV).

David knew that his heart would wander if not for the Law of the Lord. David longed in his heart to please God and fulfill His purpose for him. Yes, like all of us, he sometimes veered off course, but he was quick to repent and run back to God.

She Had His Ear

When a woman has the ear of a man, it is not to be taken lightly. While knowing what to say and when to say it is a divine attribute, it is also an act and discipline of the tongue. When God gives you the ear of your husband, your boss, or a superior, you must never use that privilege for manipulation, guile, or deceit.

This is especially true in the relationship between a husband and his wife. No one has more influence upon a man than his wife. As you pray and ask God for wisdom, the Lord will give you divine strategies to devastate the enemy's tactics to wedge a gap between you and your husband. Pray the spirit of wisdom and counsel upon your husband according to Isaiah 11:2.

Because Abigail chose to use her wisdom and her words for good, she had the ear of the servant anointed to be king.

The Prophetic Promise

The prophet Samuel was now deceased, but the prophetic promise lived on within the heart of David. Though he was not yet seated on the throne and Saul was still operating as the present king over Israel, God had rejected Saul and chosen David to lead His people Israel.

The people longed for an honest king, a prudent king who executed justice. If David was sure of anything concerning his purpose, he knew that he was called and anointed to be king not based on his own merit or stature, but based on Jehovah's word through the prophet Samuel.

David had been taken from the shepherd field and exalted as the next king. One day David would be the crowned king, ruling over all of the territories of Israel. Having witnessed through the life of Saul how a rebellious king operated, David knew the king must not take matters into his own hands but must heed God's instructions concerning the people.

Abigail took a great leap of faith to address David, and her words reminded him of God's instructions.

Minister of Defense

Abigail had become a minister of defense for Nabal. The shepherd's servants must have been thinking, *Go for it, Abigail!* David's men of armor must have thought, *Who is this woman? Wow! She has the ear of the king!*

Abigail had his ear, and she began to move forward carefully with her subtle argument. With the best interest of David and her people at heart, she helped David to see that if he didn't handle this matter properly, it could come back to haunt him in the future. The grief that would rest upon him would be great if he did not make the right move.

David had not thought this situation through. Nabal was from the tribe of Caleb. If David had acted on impulse and defended his honor by killing Nabal and the men living on his premises, then he could have alienated one of the tribes of Israel. If he had, his future task would have been to unite a divided Israel.

This one act of Abigail halted a plan that would have set him on a self-destructive course. Abigail painted a larger picture than his anger-blinded eyes had seen, and he took a broader look at the situation at hand.

Abigail's dignified diplomacy left David almost speechless. She had defused his vile anger, and now he was listening to her words of wisdom. She never presented a "resume" for the position of advisor to the king, but she suddenly found herself in that position. She had gone to the school of the Holy Spirit.

Abigail demonstrated diplomatic hospitality by providing David and his men with the food he had requested. This deed granted her favor in the sight of the future king. Though her foolish husband repaid David's request and greeting with an insult, she intervened with her customary accommodations and demonstrated God's grace by painting a word picture from her panoramic point of view.

David's Response

It was now time for the response of David, the future king.

Then David said to Abigail: "Blessed is the LORD God of Israel, who sent you this day to meet me! And blessed is your advice and blessed are you, because you have kept me this day from coming to bloodshed and from avenging myself with my own hand. For indeed, as the LORD God of Israel lives, who has kept me back from

*hurting you, unless you had hurried and come to meet me, surely
by morning light no males would have been left to Nabal!"*

*So David received from her hand what she had brought him, and
said to her, "Go up in peace to your house. See, I have heeded your
voice and respected your person."*

1 Samuel 25:32-35 NKJV

David acknowledged Abigail as a messenger sent from God and
an ambassador from heaven. Abigail's prudence and wisdom
caused David to reexamine his motives, actions, ego, and future. As
the future king of Israel, he was not to allow anger and revenge to
blind his view.

Notice that David said that God sent Abigail to him. Abigail
was not operating from her own orders or her own words. She was
marching in cadence with destiny and the perfect will of God.

Abigail's Reward

Abigail was rewarded for taking the risk in obeying God. The
woman who had given so much insight to David became his wife.
You see, Nabal died very shortly after insulting David. His life
exemplifies the truth of Mark 8:36: "What will it profit a man if he
gains the whole world, and loses his own soul?" Nabal had a stroke
and died.

David proposed to Abigail, and she accepted. David appreciated and valued her wisdom, and the story ends with Abigail as his
wife. In the Psalms, David lived to write so much wise counsel on
the subject of revenge. Could Abigail have been the person God
used to open his eyes on this topic?

Abigail had become a counselor to the king, an intercessor for her people, and a speaker of the house of God—all in one day. Promotion truly does come from the Lord!

8

PROMOTION COMES FROM THE LORD

Promotion is not guaranteed by location, experience, or education. It is based on the sovereign act of God. Even as you read this book, He can launch you in one day, with one act, with one word of wisdom from above, into the promotion He has planned for you.

Promotion is not about whom you know but to whom you belong. Promotion comes from God, and He is the One who orchestrates our lives for His good will and purpose. Before time began, He alone ordered every single step in our lives.

Abigail's life is a great example of God's promotion, and David was not offended by her elevated position of wisdom. Rather, he celebrated her as a messenger sent by God to him. Women of strength do not threaten secure men. As a man of strength and power, the future King David respected Abigail's calling and position.

A Prophet to the Nations

I can remember when I was just beginning to understand my calling and position. When God first began to bring me before prime ministers, kings, and heads of state, I had to learn how to trust in the Word of the Lord.

Abigail never expressed her personal views concerning David's policy. She simply gave him the word of the Lord as his counsel. Likewise, I could not trust in my political opinion to open these leaders' hearts. There were times when I was completely opposed to the policy of the cabinet. I had to submit to the Lord's counsel. I couldn't allow the prophetic word to be contaminated by my personal political views.

In the early '80s, I was in Kampala, Uganda. It was an intense time of seeking the Lord and interceding for this war-torn country. I will never forget Uganda in those days. The nation had suffered for a decade under one dictator after another. Mass graves filled the land, and the stench of rotting human flesh filled the air.

People had warned me not to go, but I had to obey God. We must overcome the enemy by the blood of the Lamb and by the word of our testimony and love not our lives even unto death.[1] I was clear that I had heard the call of God to go and my instruction had come expressly from heaven, so that was the strength from which I operated.

A Word From Heaven

One night I was praying about the nation, and God gave me a word for the secretary of state, who became the minister of defense. His name was Balake Kirya, and he was known as B.K. the Bishop of Parliament. He was everything that you imagine a grandfather should be. He was so loving and so full of God.

One night I prayed and interpreted my tongues and was amazed at the words that were coming out of my mouth. Here it was close to 11:00 at night, and God was instructing me concerning the head of state! My host, Zerubabel Ebangit, a former professor of economics, led me to B.K.'s house. Zerubabel was known as a man of prayer and was a minister to cannibals on an island. It was his custom to annually go away into the mountains to fast and pray for forty days.

So when Zerubabel brought me to B.K.'s house, B.K. knew there was no joking involved. B.K.'s precious wife, Grace, depicted her name through her demeanor and style. She later would become one of my mentors and teach me all the diplomatic customs of hospitality and how to approach royalty, and B.K. would become a father to me.

It was now approximately 11:45 P.M., and B.K. and Grace were about to retire for the evening. They were having their traditional English Earl Grey Tea with cream, just as the British had taught them to do during the colonial years. It was also their custom to have nightly devotions before retiring for bed.

B.K. had just prayed and informed his wife of his decision concerning his position. You see, B.K. was like Joseph. He had served for several presidential regimes. He had been imprisoned by Idi Amin and had also been in office during Obotes' and Museni's regimes. B.K. now had arthritis due to the countless nights of sleeping on damp, cold, concrete prison floors.

B.K. had prayed for so long for God to heal Uganda and to restore her to her place of honor. Uganda was once what Churchill called the "pearl of Africa," and now she looked like the ancient ruins of Rome. The potholes in the streets were so deep that a car could land in them. When I saw men pulling a car out of a pothole, I couldn't believe my eyes. I went to bed at night quoting Psalm 91 because of the rats under my bed. Uganda desperately needed healing.

Delivering the Word of the Lord

As I entered B.K.'s house, passed the security, and entered the chambers of their sitting room, I was so nervous because I knew what God had said to me. If he didn't receive it or if he thought I was flaky, what would he do to me? This was his first meeting with me, this young missionary who claimed to have the word of the Lord for the minister of defense. Who would be *my* defense if he totally disagreed with the strong warning that God was about to deliver to him?

The word came with encouragement, exhortation, edification, and correction. B.K. had been ready to resign and had put everything in place to do so. But God was not excepting his letter of resignation.

How was I to know of his situation? I opened wide my mouth, and God filled it. With accuracy the Holy Spirit gave prophetic insight and instruction to B.K. I had his ear.

It was all I could do to keep my composure as I submitted myself to the counsel of the Lord. Deep within my heart, my inner being cried out, "Not my will, but Your will be done." All I had to stand upon was the word of the Lord.

Your Gift Will Make Room for You

The Bible says that your gift will make room for you and bring you before great men.[2] Though this text of Scripture is interpreted in many ways, I believe that it means literally what it says.

In this very ripe season, do not be self-promoting or self-seeking. Your gift will make room for you. If you promote yourself before those who can make you, then they will also have the ability to break you.

B.K. fell to his knees and wept at that very moment. Not only did I have his ear, but I had his heart. B.K. favored me throughout the extent of our relationship. He became my papa, and I became his baby girl. He had intended to resign, but God reminded him that, like Caleb, he still had mountains to conquer in his ripe age.[3] He was considering his health and his age and years of suffering on behalf of his nation.

B.K. loved Uganda. She was his pearl even when no one else saw her as the pearl. He loved the people whom God had placed him over to protect. B.K. prayed day and night for his nation and was the spokesperson for Uganda and a man of integrity and honor.

God rewarded the risk I had taken for His name's sake. Whenever I was to go to Uganda, I would have diplomatic clearance. As the daughter of B.K., I rode around in a state car, had diplomatic immunity, and was treated like royalty—all because I had stepped out to obey God.

What are you waiting on before you step out of your current comfort zone to obey God's calling? There is never a perfect time to step out. As a matter of fact, God always seems to ask us to cross the Jordan while the banks are high and overflowing. On many occasions with God, you have to simply close your eyes and jump. Don't allow the what if's to haunt you and paralyze you into lethargy. Decide today to take a risk and jump into your purpose.

Abigail's Risk Won David's Heart

Abigail took a risk and assisted David in his political goals with her wisdom. A wise woman can help her husband meet his destiny. She is anointed by God to help him fulfill all that God has predestined for him. Abigail intervened and navigated David back to his moral commitments, and David saw that she possessed qualities he needed. Abigail danced her way into David's heart by appealing to his character, not his charisma.

A woman who was married to a fool became the counselor for the future king. Nabal's foolish act had not negated what God had stored up for Abigail. For years she had tried to help Nabal, and God honored her for her wisdom and faithfulness.

As a woman of strength, Abigail submitted to the order of the King of kings and was groomed for the palace unaware. What could God be grooming and preparing for you through your challenging obstacles in life? Even Jesus learned and demonstrated obedience through the things that he went through.[4]

Through years of obedience, Abigail had cultivated the character of one on whom everyone could depend. David saw this quality in Abigail and knew she could help develop and balance him in areas of his weaknesses. This is why men of strength are attracted to women of strength.

Never Deny Your Strengths

A Mediterranean proverb says, "You can't make weak men strong by making strong women weak." Women, you should never deny your strengths in order to attract a man. If he is a man of strength, he will appreciate and honor your strengths as a gift from God to bring balance to his life.

Most men, excluding fools, are aware of their weaknesses. You will be doing yourself a great disservice to try to disguise your God-given abilities and strengths in order to attract a man. Men need what you have.

I work with Arab men in predominantly Islamic regions. As I am writing this chapter, I am in Malaysia, whose population is 90 percent Islamic. Right now it is Ramadan, a holy festival to address and teach Asian male leaders. The men whom I am called to train and teach were raised in a patriarchal culture.

Couple Strength With Humility

I am always reminded when I give instruction that it is an entitled calling from God, and I do not abuse it in displaying a haughty or arrogant demeanor. I must take the position of humility coupled with strength, the traits of a true servant and minister.

Every leader must understand that he or she is only a vessel in service to the Master, the Lord Most High. Each of us must lay aside our pride, simply listen to the will of God, and obey.

When the former First Lady Hillary Clinton received words of her husband's folly, she demonstrated humility and strength in her situation. She said that as a wife she wanted to kill her husband, but as First Lady she needed to stand by the president's side. This gave me a new respect for her as a woman. She considered not her own rights or her own pain, but she deferred her rights for the greater purpose of fulfilling the need of her people. I am sure this strength coupled with humility attracted President Clinton to her from the beginning.

Abigail displayed similar strength after her husband's foolish mistake in his dealings with David. She didn't just point the finger at Nabal; she pointed at herself as well, saying, "On me, my lord, on me let this iniquity be!"

Then she pointed David toward God and his purpose. She prompted him to examine his character. The Word of the Lord had become the schoolmaster and final authority in her life, so she was able to point him back to the Law.

Abigail demonstrated the ultimate character of sobriety. Her grave counsel impressed David so much that he was never able to shake his acquaintance with her. Abigail's sensitivity and obedience ultimately brought her in the palace. Because of her obedience and her willingness to share the word of the Lord at the risk of her life, she was promoted from the wife of a fool to the wife of the beloved king.

Prayer for Wisdom

Lord, You instructed me to ask for wisdom, and You graciously promised to extend Your wisdom to me in abundance and vowed to hold back nothing. Today I need Your wisdom to help me make the right choices for my life, family, and career. Without Your wisdom I would fail, but thanks be to God who always causes me to triumph in Christ Jesus and keeps me victorious.

Father, I thank You that Your wisdom sustains me and Your knowledge increases me daily. When I need Your counsel and don't know what to do, give me understanding and the knowledge to appropriate the wisdom that lies within me that flows from Your throne room. Teach me how to reverence You in the unsupervised areas of my life. I need understanding so that I may walk in the peace of God.

You said that my heart is like deep waters, yet understanding will draw out the counsel of God from the depths of my heart for my life. Lord, give me an insatiable appetite for wisdom and show me how to search for her as choice silver so that I may have wisdom twice my age. Teach me how to be a woman of substance with sober words and how to instruct others and also receive instruction from others, because it is a wise woman that loves correction.

As I incline my ear to listen to You, I will find favor. I will watch for wisdom daily and hear instruction that will make me wise. Through wisdom I will be established. I can look back over my life and see where I erred because of the lack of wisdom. Teach me how to hold my feelings and not to be prone to vent out anger and disappointments. A wise woman builds her house with her words, and a foolish woman tears down her home with complaints. Your words of wisdom are life to all who find them; therefore, help me to make wisdom my closest friend.

Scriptures

Psalm 111:10; Proverbs 11:12; 13:10; 23:23; Isaiah 11:2; Jeremiah 10:12; Micah 6:9; 1 Corinthians 1:30; Proverbs 2:5; 8:11,33; 9:8b; 11:2,3; 15:7.

Daily Declaration

I decree that I am a woman of wisdom and I embrace correction. My character is shaped by wisdom and understanding, and I have decreed that this year I will not walk in continuous foolish errors because in the multitude of counsel I will find safety. Integrity preserves me and I hunger for truth in my inward parts. I draw out of the deep counsel of my heart by praying in the Holy Ghost daily. The divine mysteries of God are revealed to me because I have the Spirit of wisdom and revelation in the knowledge of God. God directs my path because I acknowledge Him in all of my ways.

The wisdom of God in my life makes the crooked paths straight and gives light and illumination to every obscure area of my life. I love wisdom and wisdom loves me! By wisdom I am able to walk well pleasing unto You, Lord, and You will make my enemies to be at peace with me. My lips disperse knowledge and my soft tongue of wisdom dismantles the tongue of wrath.

The wisdom of God reveals to me the path of provision for my life, the path of peace and the path of purpose. I am a wise woman increasing in wisdom daily and the integrity of remaining upright will guide me continually.

PART 4

JOCHEBED: IT'S NOT A SACRIFICE UNTIL YOU LET IT GO

9

ISRAEL'S DELIVERER IS BORN

Jochebed was a woman of great insight and vision. In the biblical record of her life her voice is never heard, yet every calculated action of Jochebed speaks louder than words. This great woman risked not only her life, but also the life of her own baby son, Moses.

> And a man of the house of Levi went and took as wife a daughter of Levi. So the woman conceived....
>
> Exodus 2:1 NKJV

The Bible tells us that Jochebed bore three children and lists the two sons first followed by the daughter.

> The name of Amram's wife was Jochebed the daughter of Levi, who was born to Levi in Egypt; and to Amram she bore Aaron and Moses and their sister Miriam.
>
> Numbers 26:59 NKJV

During her third pregnancy, Jochebed carried in her womb God's master plan for the deliverance of His people.

For over four hundred years, the Lord had been activating a plan strategically timed and powerfully purposed before the foundation of the world. By His design, Jochebed was born at the right time, in the right country, and married to the right man. She even conceived and gave birth to the proper number of children of the right genders at the appointed times and places. By God's design, she first bore a son to be Moses' ministry support. And also by His design, she bore a daughter to assist in the divine strategy to sustain Moses' life.

Slaves in Egypt

At this time, the Hebrew people dwelled in Egypt because their forefather Joseph had reigned second to Pharaoh in the land. As time passed, the Hebrews multiplied and prospered in Egypt. But their stay soon became a nightmare:

> Then a new king, who did not know about Joseph, came to power in Egypt. "Look," he said to his people, "the Israelites have become much too numerous for us. Come, we must deal shrewdly with them or they will become even more numerous and, if war breaks out, will join our enemies, fight against us and leave the country."
>
> So they put slave masters over them to oppress them with forced labor, and they built Pithom and Rameses as store cities for Pharaoh. But the more they were oppressed, the more they multiplied and spread; so the Egyptians came to dread the Israelites and worked them ruthlessly. They made their lives bitter with hard labor in brick and mortar and with all kinds of work in the fields; in all their hard labor the Egyptians used them ruthlessly.
>
> Exodus 1:8-14 NIV

Life was already difficult for the Hebrews under the tyrannical Egyptian slave masters, but before the time of Moses' birth it would become even worse. Because of the Hebrews' rapid population growth and the Pharaoh's fear that they would overrun the Egyptians, he would decree the death of every newborn male child.

Then the king of Egypt spoke to the Hebrew midwives, of whom the name of one was Shiphrah and the name of the other Puah; and he said, "When you do the duties of a midwife for the Hebrew women, and see them on the birthstools, if it is a son, then you shall kill him; but if it is a daughter, then she shall live."

Exodus 1:15,16 NKJV

The Concerns of Pregnancy

While living as slaves in the land of Egypt, joy was probably one of the last emotions a Hebrew woman felt when she discovered she was pregnant. What kind of life would she bring her child into? Worse yet, would her child live past his first breathing hours?

Imagine the feelings that must have swept over Jochebed and Amram when, after this order had been issued, they discovered she was pregnant. Amram, Moses' father, was a clan leader among the Kohathites. Now would be his time to rear his sons, passing down the leadership qualities of the Kohathites, just as his father had passed them on to him. But his dreams and ambitions for his sons were crushed by the royal decree of the king: a death order for any sons to be born of Amram or any of his people.

The Egyptian pharaohs ruled with a strong arm of dictatorship. Control was their main attribute. Indeed, the Egyptian people worshipped the pharaohs as gods.

Their Trust Was in God

Nonetheless, the children of God had been given explicit instructions to worship no other gods but the Most High alone. Surrounded by the influence of the Egyptian gods and cultural traditional practices, Amram and Jochebed had still managed to rear their children according to the Hebrew laws and customs. Their trust was in the God of their forefathers.

Furthermore, the Hebrew midwives who had been ordered to kill the male children did not comply with Pharaoh's orders. Therefore, the Hebrew women had some hope that, because of these honorable midwives, their sons would live.

> But the midwives feared God, and did not do as the king of Egypt commanded them, but saved the male children alive. So the king of Egypt called for the midwives and said to them, "Why have you done this thing, and saved the male children alive?"
>
> And the midwives said to Pharaoh, "Because the Hebrew women are not like the Egyptian women; for they are lively and give birth before the midwives come to them."
>
> Therefore God dealt well with the midwives, and the people multiplied and grew very mighty. And so it was, because the midwives feared God, that He provided households for them.
>
> Exodus 1:17-21 NKJV

However, Pharaoh's hand became fiercer toward the Hebrews. If the midwives would not kill the newborn sons, then he would still make sure the job was done. He required all of the people of Egypt to rally around his cause:

> So Pharaoh commanded all his people, saying, "Every son who is born you shall cast into the river, and every daughter you shall save alive."
>
> Exodus 1:22 NKJV

The Destiny of Israel

When we study the Bible, we see that every time God is about to send a deliverer on the scene, the enemy moves forward to attempt to destroy the promise and destiny of God's children. In the days of this diabolical decree in Egypt, the destiny of the children of Israel rested upon the willingness and obedience of one woman: Jochebed. She was carrying within her the deliverer of the nation, whose life had to be protected.

Jochebed had all of eternity's purpose pulsating within her womb. She nurtured the new life inside of her, anxiously awaiting life's birth in the midst of a decree of death. Her face was set like a flint as she anchored herself in the faith of the Most High God and refused to be moved by the external circumstances surrounding her.

As she reached the last trimester of her pregnancy, Jochebed knew the time would soon come for her child to be born. Finally, the baby lowered in her womb and became positioned for delivery. Like many mothers-to-be, Jochebed tossed and turned, restlessly anticipating the day of her child's arrival. However, Jochebed's restlessness was heightened by the anxious thoughts of bringing a child into a world that would seek his death.

Jochebed knew that her child would be sought after like a bounty hunter's prey. All the neighbors had seen her signs of pregnancy and knew that she, just like all of the other Hebrew women, would be forced to endure one of the most dreadful acts that any mother could imagine: standing helplessly by as her baby was thrown into the Nile River.

A Higher Law

Pharaoh's law said, "Every son who is born you shall cast into the river..." (Ex. 1:22 NKJV). However, Jochebed knew God's law operates independent of society, economy, culture, and location. She knew God's covenant housed within itself all of the substance and verity that made God who He was—and who He is. All of His promises are yea and amen![1] She knew external opposition could not change Him one fraction of an inch.

Jochebed felt herself operating independent of the atmospheric pressure. The law of God, His eternal covenant, causes His people to prosper in times of famine, to walk in health in the midst of an epidemic, to have peace in the midst of a storm, and to live in stability in the midst of economic collapse.

Most of us have yet to see ourselves empowered to prosper independent of our present economy, location, and environment. God promised to give us wealth—which means spiritual, emotional, mental, relational, physical, and financial abundance. If no one around believes in our vision, God has empowered us to believe and receive.[2] He has placed the ability inside of us to overcome every external obstacle. Romans 8:32 tells us that our wealth abides in us: He who did not spare His own Son shall freely give us all things.

As we cling to the vision God gives us, the difficulties of life may come to weigh us down and intimidate our dreams and visions. As we weather life's storms and adhere to the Word, disappointments and frustrations may become stronger. However, as we choose to walk in the law of God, we will see His decrees becoming our realities.

No matter how many hurdles you have to overcome, *never give up!* The laws of Pharaoh may have demanded others to give up and give in, but Jochebed refused to bow to the demands of the king.

Our lives, dreams, hopes, and visions are governed not by a set of earthly rules, but by heavenly principles. We are citizens of heaven, seated with Him in heavenly places.[3]

Jochebed refused to allow man's decree to supersede God's decree. Although all of the other women lived under the tyranny of Pharaoh's commands, Jochebed remained anchored in her faith in God. Not allowing the circumstances to make her become hopeless, she opened her heart for God's instructions to give her a way out of an impossible situation. Jochebed determined that no man would abort the future of her child.

Transforming Opposition

Jochebed did not allow Pharaoh's decrees to depress her into disparity. Instead, she transformed her opposition into destiny. As she slept under the star-filled sky, she had to have looked up and cried out in intercession for the life of her child. Her confidence was in the omnipotent One—the unfailing God. Jochebed set her trust in the eternally merciful One. Something was certainly going on between Jochebed and her God.

God's covenant promise of provision is on an individual basis. If no one else in the entire village would have chosen to trust God, Jochebed still would have. And with her individual faith, she proved to us that those who trust in the name of the Lord shall never be put to shame.[4]

What God was about to do simply because Jochebed didn't lose faith would soon change the Egyptian Empire and the future of the Hebrew nation.

Jochebed Bore a Son

Finally, the contractions began and became closer and closer.

So the woman...bore a son.

Exodus 2:2 NKJV

Ever so quietly and anxiously, Jochebed bore her son Moses into the tormented world in which she and her family lived.

Immediately after Moses' birth, Jochebed took on the unimaginably difficult task of hiding her newborn child. After taking his first breath, and before uttering his first cry, his hungry mouth was soothed with warm milk.

Every day that Jochebed nursed him, he grew. Soon, he would grow to the point that she would no longer be able to hide him. Every day, his lungs and the strength of his cry grew stronger.

Young Moses had no idea what awaited him in life, but as Jochebed nursed him to quiet his hungry cries she prayed over him. And with each prayer, a feeling grew inside of her: This child was a little different from the others.

Imagine the risk that not only she took, but that she asked her family to take. Somehow, she had to convince her older children, Aaron and Miriam, to follow her plan precisely. They watched over young Moses daily, assisting their mother in caring for him and hiding him. If Pharaoh had discovered their cooperation in this conspiracy, he would have slaughtered her whole family.

Jochebed certainly could not hang any clean diapers on the line or invite anyone to a naming ceremony or weaning celebration. And as she looked into his young eyes, she realized that he would not live with her long enough for her family to give him his bar mitzvah. She did, however, have him long enough to witness his circumcision on the eighth day, and afterward her milk comforted and quieted her baby boy.

10

LETTING GO

O nly by the help of the Lord could Jochebed gain any of these victories and the ones that would follow. As she took all of the care to hide him, she desperately sought God to receive a plan to save her child's life. As she did, her faith grew.

Knowing that she must take the utmost risk now more than ever before, Jochebed began to gather papyrus branches. A few times a day, she sent Aaron and Miriam to the Nile to fetch water, along with a few branches. Then, with detailed precision, the desperate mother weaved a basket, knowing that its strength would determine her son's safety.

Finally, after three months, the time came when Moses was too big and growing too quickly to be hidden any longer. Jochebed used tar to coat the basket she had so carefully made and positioned Moses inside of it along the reeds of the Nile. Before the excursion, Jochebed prayed one final prayer over her handsome son and launched him into the path of his destiny.

And when she saw that he was a beautiful child, she hid him three months. But when she could no longer hide him, she took an ark

of bulrushes for him, daubed it with asphalt and pitch, put the
child in it, and laid it in the reeds by the river's bank.

Exodus 2:2,3 NKJV

How Do You Let Go?

At first glance, Jochebed's decision to place her baby in a home-
made boat in the Nile seems to be an aimless, hopeless act.
However, Jochebed was behaving neither carelessly nor hopelessly.
She had prayed the whole situation into a chartered course. At that
moment, she knew that only God could maneuver the course of the
basket as well as the life it carried within.

How do you birth something so dear to you and then release it,
knowing that it is destined to die? All of Jochebed's discomfort in
pregnancy, labor, and delivery would have been for nothing but
heartbreak if Pharaoh had his way with her baby son.

But thank God the way of the Lord is sure, and the final decree
is not with man but with God. You see, before Pharaoh ever made
his royal decree to end the life of every newborn Hebrew boy, God
had need of a deliverer.

Once again, as in the days of Hagar, God had a need in the
earth. The cries of the children of Israel were coming up daily
before the Lord. Who would deliver them and be His intercessor for
His people?[1]

God had determined that enough was enough, and He had a
plan for His people. That plan would involve a woman with the
strength to surrender her very own son for His plan.

Did this woman, Jochebed, have any insight about the child she had carried in her womb for nine months? For many women, pregnancy is a time when a strong bond develops between her and her child. Many studies have shown that a child in the womb knows his or her mother's voice. Jochebed had the power to speak life to her baby, and she refused to accept death as his fate.

The power of life and death is in the tongue.[2] Jochebed must have daily spoken life-giving words over Moses. She must have prayed every day in faith for the fulfillment of God's plan for his life.

The God-ordained plan for the life of Moses began before he was ever born. God never forsakes His own. He will never allow His faithfulness to fail.[3]

We know that God has a plan for every life because He is not a respecter of persons.[4] Jeremiah 1:5 (NKJV) says, "Before I formed you in the womb I knew you; before you were born I sanctified you; I ordained you…." God has a predestined calling upon every life. However, each individual has the free will to yield to what God desires or to rebel and go his own way.

The baby Jochebed carried within her womb was marked by God to deliver His people. Before Pharaoh ever became king of Egypt, before the Egyptian Empire ever became a superpower, the Most High God willed for Moses to set His people free. The wise counsel of God premeditated Moses' actions. God looked into his future before Jochebed's water ever broke, before the first contraction ever registered in her mind, and before she released him in her handmade basket on the River Nile.

A Divine Strategy

This woman of faith and prayer, who had put her trust in her Master's ability to protect and provide for her son, followed the plan He gave her—and the results were miraculous.

And his sister stood afar off, to know what would be done to him.

Exodus 2:4 NKJV

Jochebed strategically placed her daughter where she would see exactly where Moses' boat would carry him. Did Jochebed know that the Nile fed into Pharaoh's daughter's quarters for bathing? We do not know, but we do know that Miriam watched alongside the Nile as the current of the water carried her brother.

Then, the Nile was given the order to spare the life of Moses. The moon, stars, seas, and rivers submit to God's voice. At His command, the whole earth trembles,[5] the waters divide,[6] and the sun stands still.[7] Though the Nile had claimed the life of many Hebrew infants, it would never boast the life of young Moses.

Something powerful was happening between Jochebed and her God. She saw that her Master told the sun to shine, and it bowed to His command. She witnessed that her God commanded the rain to fall, and it fell. And she was convinced that He was the same God who had the power to protect her baby.

All that God needed was for Jochebed to call upon His name for the deliverance of her child. The mourning of the other mothers who had to sacrifice their babies at the decree of Pharaoh did not alter Jochebed's determination to hide her baby and to know that God would eventually make a way of escape for him.

Into the Royal Courts

The same God who makes the wind to blow would have to breathe upon Moses after he was released from his mother's loving arms. The wind of the Holy Spirit was the driving force toward Moses' destiny, and it steered him right into the royal courts, where Pharaoh's daughter just so happened to be preparing to bathe.

Then the daughter of Pharaoh came down to bathe at the river. And her maidens walked along the riverside; and when she saw the ark among the reeds, she sent her maid to get it.

Exodus 2:5 NKJV

God honored the prayers of Jochebed and the life of the child and caused the river to bring Moses into the view of the daughter of Pharaoh. Now, just as He had turned the current of the river and made sure that nothing interrupted the princess's plans to bathe at that specific time, God would have to turn the heart of the princess whose very own father had ordered the child's death.

And when she opened it, she saw the child, and behold, the baby wept. So she had compassion on him, and said, "This is one of the Hebrews' children."

Exodus 2:6 NKJV

If the Lord had not favored Moses, he could have been a dead baby the moment he floated into the court, but the Bible says the princess had compassion on Moses. God had already placed favor in her heart, so that when she laid eyes on Moses he found favor in her sight.

She knew that he was a Hebrew baby, but some unseen force caused her to have such compassion on this baby that she was willing to revolt against her father's decree. Suddenly, because of her desire to preserve this child's well being, she had the courage to request of her father a baby who represented the very problem he was trying to eliminate. Somehow she would convince her father, and he would permit her to keep Moses.

Miriam's Role

Now it was time for Miriam, Moses' older sister, to fulfill her role in the plan Jochebed and God together had arranged. The boat's final turn into the court of the king had been Miriam's cue to get in position.

> Then his sister said to Pharaoh's daughter, "Shall I go and call a nurse for you from the Hebrew women, that she may nurse the child for you?"
>
> And Pharaoh's daughter said to her, "Go." So the maiden went and called the child's mother.
>
> Exodus 2:7,8 NKJV

Just as the princess discovered Moses, Miriam spoke up as if she had been cued. Perhaps she had rehearsed for this moment countless times with her mother at home. "Do you want me to find a Hebrew woman to nurse him?" she asked. And immediately upon the princess's command, Miriam went running back home to tell her mother that her brother was safe.

Her Son Was Safe

Panting and out of breath, Miriam struggled in her excitement to tell Jochebed all that she had witnessed. But her words only confirmed what Jochebed's heart had known: Her son was safe.

There was no way that Jochebed could have let her baby go without praying to the Lord Most High. She'd had a prayer strategy on behalf of her baby. She closed herself off from what others did and allowed God to teach her how to walk through this dark situation in His light.

Suddenly, she was witnessing a miracle: She was being beckoned to nurse the child she had just sent away into God's keeping. When the request of Pharaoh's daughter came to her, she did not need to pray about direction. Not only was she thrilled at the opportunity, but she was already seasoned in prayer.

It was not surprising that the Egyptian princess requested a Hebrew woman to become the baby's wet nurse. This practice was customary among the wealthy and royal Egyptian mothers. By employing Hebrew nursing mothers to feed their newborns, they could not only preserve their youthful and firm figures, but also avoid the constant task of responding to a hungry baby.

Jochebed was exuberant when she heard the update of Moses' welfare. Just that God had preserved him and kept him alive was worth giving God all her praise! But now to be requested to nurse her own baby was the most wonderful confirmation of God's faithfulness that she had ever witnessed.

Mother and Child Reunited

Because of Jochebed's faith and insight, God compensated her with the joy of nursing her own son!

Then Pharaoh's daughter said to her, "Take this child away and nurse him for me, and I will give you your wages." So the woman took the child and nursed him.

Exodus 2:9 NKJV

Jochebed's breasts were still filled with milk, and her body never grew weary as she fed her son. She was anxious and ready to feel her son drawing milk and life from her, his very own birth mother.

Within minutes, Jochebed found herself nursing the child she had released unto God perhaps only an hour before.

I believe that Jochebed had birthed this all in prayer, and the Master honored her request to protect and provide for her baby.

God Orchestrates Lives

If God can navigate a basket of a baby doomed for death into the household of the man who issued his death and cause the favor of God to fall upon him, He can orchestrate your life as well. Absolutely nothing is too hard for Him. Give Him praise concerning your life and anything that you are facing in your present life. He is *always* a step ahead of the enemy, and He will see you through!

I know it seems as though I am making a big fuss about the God who goes ahead of us, but we continually make Him too small in our eyes. He is bigger than anything that we could imagine or dare to dream.

God orchestrated every intricate detail for His future purpose of delivering His people out of bondage, and Jochebed was an integral part of His plan. The Egyptians were terrible slave masters of her entire Hebrew family, and because of her insight, her son would become the deliverer of them all.

Jochebed Imparted Life to Moses

Most children were nursed until they were three or four years of age. During the years of her continued relationship with Moses, Jochebed put something in him so tangible that in the years to come would make him so restless and dissatisfied with his present state that he would yield to the God of his mother. Whispering of Him to her young son, Jochebed instilled in Moses at an early age the life and covenant of the God of His people.

Jochebed Released Moses

The day came when Jochebed was required to release Moses to Pharaoh's daughter.

And the child grew, and she brought him to Pharaoh's daughter, and he became her son....

Exodus 2:10 NKJV

What a powerful lesson we all can learn from Jochebed! Because of Jochebed's obedience in letting go of her son, the cry of the children of Israel would soon come to an end. God allowed Moses to grow up in Pharaoh's house long enough to know the strategies of the pharaohs. By God's design, Pharaoh himself was training, feeding, and providing shelter for the man who would one day rise up to liberate the people he had oppressed, the children of God.

The enemy is neither all-knowing nor omnipresent. God is both, and He cleared the path for Moses. He knew the thoughts and the plans He had for his life, and His plans and prophetic pursuits were deliberate to bring Moses to a successful outcome.[8]

There is no Pharaoh in our lives powerful enough to dictate our doom. Even in a foreign land, God's people were provided for and saved by His mighty hand. And God will provide for and save us wherever we may find ourselves today.

Jochebed anchored all of her faith in this mighty God. She heard the decree from Pharaoh, yet she chose to hide her baby as long as she could to preserve him for God's purpose. Knowing a neighbor, best friend, or relative could have easily betrayed her, she hid Moses until the appointed time. Likewise, we must be willing to keep some things hidden until the appointed time.

Finally, when the appointed time came, Jochebed released Moses into the hands of God. She took her hands off of what was so dear to her. A sacrifice is never a true sacrifice until you can take your hands off of it. Jochebed truly let go and let God have His way. All she had in her possession was her faith in God, which was the most valuable commodity in her life.

God crowned Jochebed's vision and insight and rewarded her faithfulness with success. She pleased Him with her faith,[9] and Jehovah rewarded her in the most divine way. Sitting in the palace, she had nursed her son and imparted God's life into him so that when the appointed time would come, her miracle son would rise up to be the deliverer of His children.

Like Jochebed, we must anchor our confidence in the God who is mighty and powerful, the God who is majestic in all His ways. When we let go and trust God, everything that He has spoken out of His mouth will come to pass. As we keep our eyes on Him and His promise, as Jochebed did, He will crown our vision and insight and reward our faithfulness so that we arise out of every form of bondage and walk in the liberty and blessing of a life spent with Him.

Prayer for Insight and Vision

Father, You said that eyes have not seen nor have ears heard the things that You have prepared for those that love You! Yet You have determined to reveal them to me by Your Spirit. Lord, help me to develop a keen sense of discernment in my life. You said in Your Word that the mature saints develop their senses. Lord, I thank You for insight and revelation in the Spirit. Help me to walk by faith and not by sight! Assist me, Father, when I am weak. Help me not to focus in on the seen things that are only temporal and subject to change, but help me to redirect my faith into the unseen realms where things are eternal.

Help me to see with my spiritual eyes what my natural eyes cannot see. Help me to hope against all odds and give me a confidence when there are things that I know are of You. Father, teach me how to train my human spirit to become more sensitive to You and Your unctioning. Cause my ears to hear a word saying, "This is the way, walk ye in it!"

I thank You, Lord, that You are guiding me perpetually and Your calm vision sees what I cannot see. As the Spirit of God searches my mind, I submit to the Holy Spirit's guidance because He is the Spirit of Truth and He has been given to me as a gift, promise, helper, and teacher; He shows me things to come. When I don't know what to do and what to pray, the Holy Spirit makes groanings that cannot be uttered in articulate speech.

Thank You, Father, for giving me the promise of the Spirit, who helps me when I need Him the most. Lord, help me to rely upon and depend heavily upon the Holy Spirit when I am attempting to do things on my own. Holy Spirit, I welcome You into my life as my ultimate teacher in life. Teach me the ways of the Father, and reveal and expose the deep things of His heart to my heart.

Holy Spirit, teach me to recognize the voice of the Spirit and the way of the Spirit. You, Father, promised me that You would reveal the mysteries of Your will for my life. Every hindering plot of the enemy is exposed and revealed to me through the Holy Spirit. Lord, I thank You that I don't have to be led about like a horse with a bit in his mouth, because the Spirit of the living God leads me. Thank You, Holy Spirit, for giving me spiritual understanding into the knowledge of God's ways. Thank You, Lord, that I not only speak, but I comprehend and understand the wisdom of God. Lord, I thank You that the Holy Spirit reveals the hidden wisdom of God that has been hidden for me from the beginning.

Lord, I thank You that for every obscure area of my life, Your wisdom and revelation brings understanding and illumination. I thank You that I don't have to walk in darkness or confusion because You always light my path through Your Word. Lord, give me vision for my future. You promised me that if I would not lean to my own comprehension and understanding and if I would allow You to interpret my course, that You would direct my path. Therefore I trust in You, Lord, with all of my heart. I ask You to help me, Holy Spirit, to acknowledge the Lord in all of my ways.

Scriptures

Joshua 2; Luke 7:36; Exodus 1; Acts 5:29; Matthew 9:20-22.

Daily Declaration

I decree that I am a woman of vision; even though my vision is tarrying I will wait for it. Although I cannot see in the natural the full vision for my life and ministry, I know that my Father has begun a good work in me. This good work in me is for the express purpose of fulfilling the established work of the ministry.

Holy Spirit, I decree that You are my ultimate helper and teacher, and I look to You daily for my guidance. Every time I get a check in my spirit I will yield to Your unctionings. I decree that I have the Spirit of wisdom and revelation operating in my life on a continual basis. The Lord is speaking to me at all times, and I know and hear and follow His voice.

I build up myself on my most holy faith by praying in the Holy Ghost. I purpose to develop my sensitivity to the things of the Spirit. I bring my outward man under subjection so that my inward man will increase. I acknowledge my need and dependency upon the Word of God, which is the living instrument that the Holy Spirit agrees with in fulfilling the plan of God for my life.

As I develop insight and wisdom, I will walk in a place of confidence knowing the will of the Lord for my life. I know the hope of my calling and I have spiritual insight into the ways of God continually.

PART 5

THE DAUGHTERS OF ZELOPHEHAD: "WE WILL NOT BE DENIED AT THE GATE"

11

FIVE SISTERS UNITE

God used the daughters of Zelophehad to be history makers. Their lives exemplify courage, temperance, and patience. They are introduced to us in Numbers 26, where we learn that their father was a godly man who had five daughters but no sons.

Zelophehad son of Hepher had no sons; he had only daughters, whose names were Mahlah, Noah, Hoglah, Milcah and Tirzah.

Numbers 26:33 NKJV

These five daughters of Zelophehad had very interesting names: Mahlah, Noah, Milcah, Hoglah, and Tirzah. The meanings of these names immediately raise questions about the circumstances surrounding each of their births.

Mahlah, the name of the firstborn, means sickly or weak. Perhaps she was very sick at birth. By contrast, the name of the next daughter, Noah, means rest and comfort. Perhaps the birth of a healthy baby brought the girls' parents rest and comfort. The name of the third daughter, Hoglah, means partridge. Following Hoglah was Milcah, whose name means counselor. Perhaps she was a strong messenger of the word of the Lord and delivered sound advice. Finally came Tirzah, whose name means benevolent and pleasing.[1]

From the text, we know the father of these five women was a faithful man of character and principle. For example, when a man named Korah led a rebellion against God's anointed leader, Moses, Zelophehad remained faithful to him.[2]

A Policy for Distributing Land

Israel was approaching the final stages of the long journey out of Egypt, into the Promised Land. Now at God's leading, Moses instated a policy for distributing portions of the land of promise among the people of Israel.

> The LORD said to Moses, "The land is to be allotted to them as an inheritance based on the number of names. To a larger group give a larger inheritance, and to a smaller group a smaller one; each is to receive its inheritance according to the number of those listed. Be sure that the land is distributed by lot. What each group inherits will be according to the names for its ancestral tribe. Each inheritance is to be distributed by lot among the larger and smaller groups."

Numbers 26:52-56 NIV

The interpretation of this law was based on a parochial structure, in which the inheritance was passed down from father to son. It also called for the son to take care of his mother and unmarried sisters. However, the present interpretation of the law was inequitable because it excluded women who had no brother, father, or husband.

The Girls Had To Fight

Because Zelophehad had no sons, his offspring would be exempt from the portion of land to which he was entitled. When he died in the journey passage to Canaan, his daughters realized that their father's name and portion would now be cut off forever.

The girls had no alternative but to fight for what they felt was rightfully due them. If they themselves did not speak on their behalf, their father's portion would be taken away and his name forgotten.

Out of the five sisters, not one was married. The easiest way to enjoy the benefits of inherited land would have been to marry into the inheritance of another man. This would have been the path of least resistance toward attaining the privileges of an inheritance. Not only could they have gained access to their husbands' portions, but if they bore sons, they would also have access to their sons' inheritance as long as they lived.

Tradition alone would have forced them to marry, but these five girls were not bound to tradition. Neither were they driven to merely attain land. Their desire was to maintain the honor of their father's name and to attain what was rightfully due him and his bloodline.

Therefore, in agreement and on one accord, the five sisters determined to fight for their father's portion. No one had ever dared to openly question the law, but now these five sisters determined not to keep silent any longer.

Developing a Strategy

But first they had to have a strategy. They needed not only to speak out, but to choose the right time and the right audience.

Solomon teaches us that there is a time and a purpose for everything: There is even "a time to keep silence, and a time to speak" (Eccl. 3:7 NKJV). The fact that he first mentions silence indicates that we must first keep silent and think things through thoroughly before we take advantage of the time to speak, for there is certainly a time to speak.

We must seek God first to discover what to say and how to say it. Some things need not be said except to Him alone in prayer. Sometimes the hardest thing to do is to remain silent on a matter that we feel needs desperately to be addressed. However, sometimes God simply wants us to intercede so that when the change comes, He receives the glory.

Furthermore, instead of us winning the debate or getting our point across, He desires to get His point across through us. Believe it or not, there is a higher satisfaction and fulfillment than the victory gained from winning an argument. It comes from allowing God to have His way by silencing ourselves and giving His words full rein.

United for God's Cause

In the case of the five daughters of Zelophehad, God was in the midst of their confrontation. It was the mind of God to demonstrate equity and also to exemplify our spiritual inheritance in Christ Jesus. We know that in Christ the laws of inheritance are not based on a patriarchal legal structure, but rather on a covenant that extends to everyone—male or female, Jew or Gentile, slave or free.[3]

The women had to come to a place of unity to fight for this cause. If one fought against the other, the power would be weakened because one of the links in the chain would be broken.

Through these five sisters, God powerfully displayed unity among women. How often we hear, "It's so hard to get women to work together." However, the Master proved this wrong through the cooperation of the daughters of Zelophehad. These five women bonded together to fight for the preservation of their father's inheritance. In harmony, they pulled together to achieve a common goal, and as a result they all obtained the victory.

Of course, each sister's contribution made their efforts an overall success. However, they had to come into the power of agreement. They had to believe that they were doing the right thing, that they were all entitled to a designated portion. They had to agree to keep their opinions to themselves until it was time to address the matter. And, finally, they had to agree to fight together until the end.

They refused to allow the laws that were established to keep them from their heart-driven purpose. Something inside of them refused to allow legislative systems and decisions to prohibit them from rising up to attain their rightful portion. Something inside of them screamed, "It is not right to forget our father and deny us just because he did not have sons!"

As a result, they made a plan for change. They had not come this close to the land of inheritance to witness everyone else receiving their allotted portions and to be denied at the gate of the city. To come so far, to go through so much, and now to be told that they could not have what others had simply because they were women was not an option for them!

A Proper Pursuit

Although they were determined to claim their rights, the girls kept their mouths closed until the appointed time. They didn't spend their time complaining to their neighbors. Only at the proper time did they go, following the proper procedure and meeting with the proper audience.

Their first audience, of course, was God. Then, following the channels orchestrated by Moses, they made their case known before the rulers of their people. They waited patiently, followed proper protocol, and refused to be denied until Moses heard their case.

> *Mahlah, Noah, Hoglah, Milcah, and Tirzah...stood before Moses, before Eleazar the priest, and before the leaders and all the congregation, by the doorway of the tabernacle of meeting....*
>
> Numbers 27:1,2 NKJV

All five sisters were standing before the entire counsel at the doorway of the tabernacle of meeting. They had all been incubating this message in their spirits, and now was the time to deliver their appeal and to stand in faith that God would be their defense.

The Daughters' Appeal

The five daughters of Zelophehad began their appeal by reminding Moses of their father's integrity and reputation. They said, "Our father died in the wilderness; but he was not in the company of those who gathered together against the LORD, in company with Korah..." (v. 3 NKJV).

Second, they presented a question that must have caught the rulers off guard: "Why should the name of our father be removed from among his family because he had no son?..." (v. 4 NKJV). Perhaps Moses had never considered a case like this, in which a man's rightful land allotment would be forfeited just because he had no sons.

Finally, the five sisters brought their closing statement before the prophets and priest: "...Give us a possession among our father's brothers" (v. 4). They knew their uncles would receive the land apportioned to them; but without some merciful intervention, their father's inheritance would be lost.

The Bible says that we have not because we ask not.[4] These five sisters were not afraid to ask. They spoke to their mountain[5] and refused to be intimidated. They would not be silent just because they were women. They didn't ask to be born women. That was God's idea, and their courage would soon prove to be a fruitful act for Him.

12

A VOICE FOR THE VOICELESS

Once the five sisters made their request, Moses had to go to God for the answer. He had learned that he could not mediate for God's people on his own terms. "So Moses brought their case before the LORD" (v. 5 NKJV).

God always speaks up for His women, and He spoke to Moses directly on behalf of these five women who had shown such temperance and patience waiting for the divine time to approach the rulers. The opening statement from the Lord was one of deliverance for the daughters of Zelophehad.

And the LORD spoke to Moses, saying: "The daughters of Zelophehad speak what is right; you shall surely give them a possession of inheritance among their father's brothers, and cause the inheritance of their father to pass to them."

Numbers 27:6-8 NKJV

This was no small matter! God showed up for the daughters and validated their request. He told the prophet that what they were speaking was right. Their father's faithfulness and their silent preparations were now being rewarded openly. The Lord commanded Moses to give them a possession of their father's inheritance.

Paving the Way for Women

Not only were these women's lives affected, but their bold request paved the way for an equitable interpretation of the law. God continued speaking to Moses, saying:

> *"And you shall speak to the children of Israel, saying: 'If a man dies and has no son, then you shall cause his inheritance to pass to his daughter. If he has no daughter, then you shall give his inheritance to his brothers. If he has no brothers, then you shall give his inheritance to his father's brothers. And if his father has no brothers, then you shall give his inheritance to the relative closest to him in his family, and he shall possess it.' And it shall be to the children of Israel a statute of judgment, just as the LORD commanded Moses."*
>
> Numbers 27:8-11 NKJV

Their case was met with opposition—but not by the rulers. It came from within their family. The chief fathers of the families of their grandfather came before Moses with their challenge.

> *"Now if they are married to any of the sons of the other tribes of the children of Israel, then their inheritance will be taken from the inheritance of our fathers, and it will be added to the inheritance of the tribe into which they marry; so it will be taken from the lot of our inheritance. And when the Jubilee of the children of Israel comes, then their inheritance will be added to the inheritance of the tribe into which they marry; so their inheritance will be taken away from the inheritance of the tribe of our fathers."*
>
> Numbers 36:3,4 NKJV

The only concern their uncles had was that if they married into another tribe, then their brother Zelophehad's portion would be given to another man's tribe. Their concern set the stage for a new proclamation. Moses was commanded to go to the entire congregation to speak to the children of Israel concerning the new law instituted for women.

> Then Moses commanded the children of Israel according to the word of the LORD, saying: "What the tribe of the sons of Joseph speaks is right. This is what the LORD commands concerning the daughters of Zelophehad, saying, 'Let them marry whom they think best, but they may marry only within the family of their father's tribe.' So the inheritance of the children of Israel shall not change hands from tribe to tribe, for every one of the children of Israel shall keep the inheritance of the tribe of his fathers. And every daughter who possesses an inheritance in any tribe of the children of Israel shall be the wife of one of the family of her father's tribe, so that the children of Israel each may possess the inheritance of his fathers. Thus no inheritance shall change hands from one tribe to another, but every tribe of the children of Israel shall keep its own inheritance."
>
> Numbers 36:5-9 NKJV

A Law Providing for Everyone

God not only rewarded the five women with their allotments, but as a just judge He decreed a law of inheritance with a defense clause for women. Now women did not have to have brothers or be married in order to benefit from the allotments of the land. God decreed a law that provided for everyone. No one would be exempt from His goodness.

Women in generations to come would now be compensated because of the determined and bold faith of these women to wait on God for the appointed time to go to the top to be heard.

Like the daughters of Zelophehad, we carry in our spirits a plan and purpose from the Almighty to bless our generation. God is waiting for people who will be His mouthpiece in the earth for those who cannot defend their own case. He is looking for women intercessors. We have been called to the ministry of reconciliation, to stand in the gap between humanity and the redeeming Lord. We have within us the power to fight the good fight of faith.[1]

God needs women in the body who will not be satisfied with tea parties and women's fellowships that only bless and minister to each other. It is time to take the water to the desert and stop taking the water to the ocean! Over two billion women and children around the world suffer. It is time for us to plead their case before our Lord and fight for them to be allotted a portion of their inheritance. We have all been blessed, and it is now time to use our voice for those who have no voice.

As we hear His voice, we will become a voice for those who have no voice. It is now time to speak up for what is right, and the Lord shall be our defense. As history makers and world changers, we must rise up! It is time to possess not only our land, but also the land of those denied at the gate!

Claiming the Inheritance

When the time came for the children of Israel to possess the Promised Land, the five women made their case once again. They stood before Eleazar the priest and the rulers, as before—except that Moses' successor, Joshua, now stood in his place:

Mahlah, Noah, Hoglah, Milcah, and Tirzah...came near before Eleazar the priest, before Joshua the son of Nun, and before the rulers, saying, "The LORD commanded Moses to give us an inheritance among our brothers." Therefore, according to the commandment of the Lord, he gave them an inheritance among their father's brothers. Manasseh's share consisted of ten tracts of land besides Gilead and Bashan east of the Jordan, because the daughters of the tribe of Manasseh received an inheritance among the sons.

Joshua 17:3-6 NKJV

Like defense attorneys in the courtroom settling a dispute over property distribution, these girls knew the law and claimed the property on the east side of the Jordan. This was where the land was pliable and fruitful. These five sisters were wise negotiators.

God Waits for Us To Possess the Promise

The assertiveness of these five women teaches us that we are not waiting on God, but God is waiting on us to possess the land of promise, our rightful inheritance. What we learn to live with will ultimately shape, mold, and limit our potential. But a life in Christ Jesus launches us beyond our natural ability to reach for the promise of God.

God had a plan for the five sisters, and they stood together believing that the Lord was on their side. All odds were against them, but they had nothing to lose. The interpretation of the laws had already taken everything from them.

Like these five women, we must be willing to pursue the promise God's way. The girls chose to do it God's way, and they ended up receiving God's results. They came together as one, went through the proper chain of command, went to the top, and spoke only at the appointed time about their common objective. Finally, because of their temperance and willingness to wait for the proper time, they won their case and recovered their rightful portion.

Intercessors for Generations To Come

God used these five women to be history makers and world changers. They refused to be denied at the gate and fought for what would be a blessing for generations to come. They became the intercessors for deprived women in the entire Hebrew nation—not just for their own season, but for generations to come.

In life, we must always remember that our battles for what is right are never to benefit us only. What we go through, we also endure for others coming behind us.

I am writing this chapter in India, where over one billion people live. I am sitting at the foothill of a massive mountain. As I have looked around this nation, I can see the result of Ghandi's struggles. The people of India live today as benefactors of his obedience.

Similarly, as an African American, I now enjoy the benefits that Martin Luther King fought so severely for. His obedience altered history and changed legislation and benefited every following generation. Millions of people reaped the reward for this one man's willingness to speak up for those whose voices had not been heard.

Projecting His Voice for Those Without a Voice

Now I find myself in a position to help others whose voices have not been heard. I have worked in developing nations for over twenty years in male-dominated nations where there are no laws to defend women, fight for women, or simply honor their right to exist. In many regions of the world today, women are automatically denied the privileges that men are afforded.

In many African cultures today, if a woman's husband dies, her in-laws can whisk away everything that the couple struggled together to obtain. The sister-in-law can then live in the house that the wife labored to help provide for her family. The wife and her children are then ordered to leave with, in many cases, no possessions. All this can happen even if the in-laws never helped her husband in life.

In some Eastern cultures and in remote regions of Kenya, when a man dies the wife is obligated to marry his brother. I can remember a story of a young man and woman who had four children, and the wife had completed nursing school. The young couple worked hard and sacrificed together as young parents. The husband died, and the young woman was faced with controlling in-laws who demanded that she leave her church and return to the remote village and marry his brother.

The challenge that faced the bewildered bride was beyond anything that we could imagine. The brother was an alcoholic and an unbeliever. He was still practicing tribal beliefs and customs and had other wives. The tradition states that on the night of the day of the husband's death, the wife is ordered to sleep with her brother-in-law to preserve the dead brother's seed.

Lonely and afraid, she ran to her pastor, who was my friend, and lived in the metropolitan city of Namibia. The believers helped her to escape with the children. I will never forget the indescribable desperation she expressed as she pled with me to pray for her.

This is exactly what God wants to do in this season of our lives. He is looking for women who will rise up out of mediocrity, apathy, ease, and complacency and project His voice in the earth. When we make our request to God, He always hears us when we pray.[2]

Reach for Every Blessing

When we rise up inside and decide to reach for every blessing for which the Father God offered the blood of Jesus, all of heaven will back us. We don't have to be sick, denied, bound, or held back any longer. A price has been paid to purchase our inheritance, but we must go in and possess and claim what is rightfully our portion.

There are forces that daily endeavor to prohibit us from taking our possessions, but we must agree with what God has said. Rise up and decide that you will no longer lack when provision has been made. Stand up and refuse to be denied what is rightfully yours.

I had to decide that I would not be denied ministry in the Middle East because I am a woman. Nor will I be denied because I am unmarried, or because I am an African American, or for any other reason that any human could come up with.

God proclaimed my assignment to teach men who have never taken instructions from a woman before. In some of the Arabic countries that I work in, a five-year-old boy can tell his mother what to do because he is a male and the mother does not chastise him because she is a female.

But at the same time that God proclaimed my gender and ethnicity, He proclaimed my liberty and assignment. Just as He does with everyone, He called me before He formed the earth. And He knew when He called me that I would be born a woman. He knew that when I would answer the call, I would be unmarried. And, of course, He knew that I would be an African American born in North Carolina!

It was His job to take this part of my persona and orchestrate it to complement my calling. Everything I'd been told would be my hindrances, God has used as a novelty. Now when I instruct men in male-dominated cultures, at first they scratch their heads, but then they follow my instruction. Only God could open these men's hearts by overriding the social rules of their land.

It Is Harvest Time

Regardless of man-made laws or social rules, the laws that govern the heavens and earth remain the same. God's laws are covenant principles established for our good. He designed them that it may be well with us.[3]

We must believe like the daughters of Zelophehad that it is our season of inheritance. It is our harvest time, and we have a right to receive our blessings. If anyone is going to be a recipient of redemption's entitlements, it might as well be me—and it might as well be you!

The birthing of your ministry, business, future, and marriage lies within you. The same God of peace who watched over the daughters of Zelophehad is the God who will watch over you. He will not allow one of His sovereign plans for you to fall to the ground. According to Proverbs 5:21, you are "ever before the eyes of the LORD, and He ponders all [your] paths."

You will fulfill all that He has assigned to you. Contrary to the demeaning opinions of others, God is exalting you high above your enemies, placing your feet on higher ground, and enlarging your boundaries.[4]

No More Postponement

God will not always erase the enemies, but He will bless you in spite of their decrees. He will increase you so much in their midst and make such an open show of them that they will be put to shame in your midst.[5]

As you read this, ponder the areas of your life that you rightfully have a promise from God to obtain. This day refuse to live in denial and delay. You will not be denied. Your days of denial are over, and this is your day of jubilee.

Ezekiel 12:28 (NKJV) declares, "None of My words will be postponed any more, but the word which I speak will be done." There will be no more postponement in your life—not another year, not another day. You have a right to be healed and a right to be prosperous. You have a right to walk in peace. You a have a right to fulfill your calling and obey God, who will fulfill what He has promised you. If unbelief and fear sit at the gate and combat your faith to rob you from your inheritance, resist them and ask the Father to increase your capacity to receive what He has provided for you.

Have you died to your dreams, visions, and hopes while waiting to enter in? Zelophehad died in the journey while waiting to enter the Promised Land. He had been a Hebrew slave in Egypt and lived under years of oppression from Pharaoh and was with those who crossed the Red Sea. He even held on when others rebelled against Moses. Yet he died waiting to enter in because, like the rest of his generation, he lost faith and hope of the promise.[6]

Resurrect your faith and hope for the promise. Your days of waiting are over. God has proclaimed *no postponement* for you! You don't have to be denied any longer, for any reason! You can declare that you are willing to pay any price to see God's decree for your life executed this day.

Your ministry is waiting to be born. The husband whom you have believed for is waiting to enter your life. Your promotion is waiting to be handed to you. You can decide now that you won't be denied another year. You can decree before your God that the Lord will increase you more and more, according to Psalm 115:14.

All of heaven is waiting to accommodate you and support you. Like the five daughters of Zelophehad, rise up and refuse to be denied at the gate in any area of your life. Today, declare your covenant rights, and prepare to possess the promise—not only for yourself or your own generation, but for all those you represent as you pursue your rightful inheritance.

Prayer for Temperance and Divine Timing

Father, I thank You that I am learning to place my hand over my mouth when I am urged to speak out. I thank You that You teach me how to wait on You and walk in cadence with Your divine timing because Your timing is equal to Your purpose. Father, I must admit that it is not always easy or convenient to harness my thoughts and restrain my tongue. Your Word tells me in Ecclesiastes that there is a time to speak and a time to refrain from speaking. Give me discernment and wisdom to know when to speak and when to hold what You have revealed to me in confidence and take the revealed matters to You in prayer.

Father, as You reveal the hidden secrets of the enemy to me, please keep me in a position of sobriety and make me steadfast and unmovable. Lead me by Your Spirit, Oh Lord, and cause my human spirit to become more and more sensitive to Your proddings. Don't allow me to move outside of Your sovereign will. Keep me harnessed to only walk in the stages that You have ordained for my life. I thank You, Father, that the Holy Spirit is working in me daily and teaching me how to listen and how to be still. I thank You that with clarity I will know what to do, when to do it, where to go, and when to go. I will know in intricate details what to say and when to say it. I thank You that I think twice before I speak and I ponder my words carefully.

I thank You, Lord, for working in me by the power of the Holy Spirit to shape and mold my character. I thank You for the peaceable fruit of righteousness. I thank You that I am a covenant woman who is perpetually led by the Holy Spirit daily. I am a self-controlled woman who walks in the fruit of temperance, and nothing and no one forces me to react ungodly. I live from the inside out and I receive my instructions from the Holy One. I refuse to live by the empty promises of man. God who has validated me before time began initiates my intents and motives. I am not in a hurry nor do I live in anxiety. God has determined my life before time began and orchestrates the stages of my destiny to ensure that they all come into fruition at their appointed time.

Scriptures

1 Timothy 3:2-5; Titus 2:2; Romans 13:14; 1 Corinthians 9:25; Philippians 4:5; 1 Thessalonians 5:6; 2 Peter 1:5.

Daily Declaration

I confess that I am a woman who does not have to be led about like a horse with a bit in its mouth, but I willingly submit to the mandates of heaven. My life is in the hand of God's divine providence. My life is the glove and His sovereign will is the hand that fits the glove. The urgency of providence is God's method for fulfilling His original plan for me. I walk in sync with His timing, and I do not move ahead of God nor do I move too slowly. Daily I yield to His mighty hand, and the armies of heaven are warring on my behalf to bring into fruition all that the Master has ordained for my life. Because of my confidence in Him who has begun this good work in me, I can walk in temperance and self-control. I do not move hastily because it is the counsel of the Lord that will ultimately stand. Psalm 135:6 declares that whatsoever the Lord pleases, that He does in heaven, and in the earth, and in the deep places.

Lord, I thank You that I am adding to my faith self-control and to the fruit of self-control I add knowledge. On one side I have knowledge, and on the other side I am instructed in 2 Peter 1:6 to add perseverance to my self-control. One attribute reveals to me how You restrain me, and the other attribute of perseverance reveals how to maintain and uphold me. I refuse to give up or operate in laziness for I am focused and live a life of purpose.

PART 6

DEBORAH:
GOD SENDS AWAITED HELP

13

WIFE, JUDGE, PROPHETESS, AND WARRIOR

In a time of great military oppression, after twenty years of torment, Israel cried out to God for help.[1] Our Master is a present help in time of trouble.[2] Israel had fallen into this trouble because of their own sin, but regardless of the folly of man, the Lord will never shut His ear to repentant hearts. Our help comes from the Lord.[3]

God heard His children crying out to Him from under the oppression of Canaan's King Jabin. As a result, He raised up a mother to intervene in defense of His children.

Now Deborah, a prophetess, the wife of Lapidoth, was judging Israel at that time. And she would sit under the palm tree of Deborah between Ramah and Bethel in the mountains of Ephraim. And the children of Israel came up to her for judgment.

Judges 4:4,5 NKJV

Years of judging matters had taught Deborah how to hear from God with detailed specificity. Case after case, year after year, Deborah had judged righteously. Frustrated and anguished people desperate for resolve came to her, which sharpened her patience and discernment.

It was this discernment and spiritual sensitivity that she depended on to lead her people out from under their oppression. The mystery of God was about to unfold, for He always reveals His ways to those who hunger and thirst after righteousness, those willing to obey Him. Her maternal instinct worked in conjunction with the Holy Spirit's stirring within her to prepare a strategy to protect the children of Israel.

Divine Marching Orders

When Deborah had received her instructions from heaven, she immediately acted on His plan.

> *Then she sent and called for Barak the son of Abinoam from Kedesh in Naphtali, and said to him, "Has not the* LORD *God of Israel commanded, 'Go and deploy troops at Mount Tabor; take with you ten thousand men of the sons of Naphtali and of the sons of Zebulun; and against you I will deploy Sisera, the commander of Jabin's army, with his chariots and his multitude at the River Kishon; and I will deliver him into your hand'?"*

> Judges 4:6,7

God anoints people to fulfill assignments and to execute His sovereign plan in the earth until it reflects heaven's pattern, and He had anointed Deborah for the task of delivering His marching orders to Barak. Barak was not a weak or timid man, yet he traveled from the north to seek counsel from the prophetess of Israel. Traditional and cultural gender roles had to bow their knee to the anointing.

Israel's mother was confident in her orders. Without a trace of timidity or instability in her voice, this woman of strength and faith confidently executed the command of her Master. When Barak arrived, he immediately submitted to her prophetic insight. This strong commander, highly ranked, mature, and proven, submitted to Deborah's strategy of war simply because he knew that she was anointed for the assignment. She had already heard every strategy from heaven to conquer the armies of Canaan. He knew her war tactics were sound because she had heaven's stamp of approval.

"Not Without You, Deborah!"

However, Barak, a man so secure in times past, did not hesitate to reveal to Deborah his concerns. Though she told him of God's covenant oath to give him victory over Sisera, every piece of natural evidence predicted a completely different outcome—namely, his defeat.

Sisera was experienced in surveying and analyzing and destroying his enemies' potential. Nevertheless, the word of the Lord was all Barak needed to lead his men into battle. The Lord had given His word that He would lure Sisera and the army of Jabin into his midst, thus allowing Barak to ambush his opponent.

Rest in the Word of the Lord

You may not be able to see how the Master could ever accomplish the fulfillment of your request. But rest in the Word of the Lord, and it shall never fail. Stand upon His promises until rest comes for you. Go to battle in prayer and intercession with the Word of the Lord.

In order for the enemy to win over you, he would have to be ahead of God, the Originator and the Source of life itself. His wisdom and knowledge would have to supersede God's. He would have to have been there before the creation of the heavens and the earth, before the foundations of time. He would have to reverse the creation of life and time and abort every detailed plan of the Godhead in order to stop your future. And we know that this is impossible! In order for the enemy to be ahead of you, he would have to be ahead of God, because God has engrafted you in the palm of His hand. Your plans were established before time began:

> *Who has saved us and called us with a holy calling, not according to our works, but according to His own purpose and grace which was given to us in Christ Jesus before time began.*
>
> 2 Timothy 1:9 NKJV

God equipped us with all that we need to succeed in life and has given all things that pertain to life and godliness.[4] Then He told us exactly how to succeed in life—by reading, thinking about, and doing His Word:

> *This Book of the Law shall not depart from your mouth, but you shall meditate in it day and night, that you may observe to do according to all that is written in it. For then you will make your way prosperous, and then you will have good success.*
>
> Joshua 1:8 NKJV

Then He gives us an anchor to stabilize us in the midst of the battle. That anchor is wisdom. "Wisdom and knowledge will be the stability of your times…" (Isa. 33:6 NKJV).

When God promises to give the enemy into your hands, what more do you need? When God says it, all you need to do is believe it and it is done.[5] Regardless of our visual perception of the matter, God's Word is final!

Still, Barak requested some reassurance:

And Barak said to her, "If you will go with me, then I will go; but if you will not go with me, I will not go!"

Judges 4:8 NKJV

Barak needed Deborah to go with him into battle. Perhaps he wasn't as secure in his relationship with God as she was.

When a Man Reveals His Weaknesses

When a man trusts a woman enough to reveal his weaknesses, as Barak did, she should never uncover his weaknesses. Of course, if he is in deliberate, continual sin, she must address it—but she should do so with integrity and confidentiality. If a husband shares with his wife his weaknesses, for example, her godly life can influence him to mature and change, as 1 Peter 3:1-2 (NKJV) says.

Wives, likewise, be submissive to your own husbands, that even if some do not obey the word, they, without a word, may be won by the conduct of their wives, when they observe your chaste conduct accompanied by fear.

Many people think, *Nobody can change anyone!* However, God has continually used the modeled lifestyles of individuals of prayer and character to provoke, convict, and even humble others.

It isn't easy to lead the life of submission necessary to help God change others, but He is there to help us grow. He who began a good work in us shall complete it, even until the day of Christ Jesus.[6] God never starts anything that He is unable to complete, but we must be willing to yield to His way. This is a great battle, especially for those who are naturally self-willed and strongly opinionated. However, only when we allow God to work in us can He work through us.

Barak Requested the Specialist

Barak revealed his weakness in faith to Deborah. His skill and ability rested in his military tactics and his years of infantry training. But for the presence of the Lord and the keen sense of spiritual insight, he requested the specialist—Deborah.

Deborah had proven to have the ear of God. She displayed confidence due to an ear anointed to hear from the Master on a daily basis. Deborah had no fear, not even of Sisera. Her confidence was in the name of the Lord.

It was because of her confidence that Barak, a man of great military stature, refused to go to battle without Deborah, God's mouthpiece. Deborah listened to Barak's request, pondered his words, and responded with profound wisdom. Knowing that Barak had spoken from his heart, Deborah said,

> *"I will surely go with you; nevertheless there will be no glory for you in the journey you are taking, for the LORD will sell Sisera into the hand of a woman...."*

> Judges 4:9 NKJV

Barak Was Willing To Decrease

A victory over Jabin's army would have looked impressive on Barak's military record. However, though her words challenged his ego, he quickly aligned his focus with hers. Their people needed deliverance, and he was willing to decrease to allow the plan and purpose of God to unfold.

God's word to Israel was that He would give Sisera into their hands. Barak's logic had to bow to the way of the Lord. His faith was not as seasoned as Deborah's was, so he anchored his faith in her faith in God's word. Barak's position was quite simple: He was not going into battle without Deborah! If she didn't go, he wouldn't go!

Marching Into Battle

Deborah had made the decision to go with Barak, and she followed through with confidence.

> ...Then Deborah arose and went with Barak to Kedesh. And Barak called Zebulun and Naphtali to Kedesh; he went up with ten thousand men under his command, and Deborah went up with him.
>
> Judges 4:9,10 NKJV

The mother of Israel stood beside Barak and an army of ten thousand. As the Lord had commanded, they headed toward Mount Tabor.

Deborah was clear about her instructions from God, which is vital for a woman who steps outside of the roles traditionally placed on her. The restrictive traditional gender roles in the patriarchal age were enough to intimidate any woman, but Deborah's validation came from God.

Self-Appointed Critics

As Deborah departed for Mount Tabor, surely self-appointed critics questioned her decision. Most of these people had never won a battle in their own lives. Generally, self-appointed critics tell others how to do what they themselves have never in their lives done.

Another word for a self-appointed critic is "backbiter." The reason they are called backbiters is that they don't have the courage to bite up front. Instead of confronting a person face-to-face, they find human garbage disposals and throw their trash of criticism and strife into their open ears. They spend their lives focusing on other people's accomplishments, while never achieving their own goals.

Even if critics pointed scornfully at Deborah, she was in the army now. Whether others liked it or not, her focus was on saving the lives of her people. She didn't allow anyone's opinion to distract her from her focus. She remained steadfast in her assignment.

Likewise, our aim as women of God is to focus on our divine assignment. Our job is not to step out of our battle march to answer to or defend ourselves against those who don't celebrate our calling. Our job is to stay in step, listening only to our heavenly commander's call.

14

BALANCING

Deborah's boldness was certainly commendable, but her husband's obedience and willingness to release his wife and his faith and belief in her calling were also very commendable. Judges 4:4 (NKJV) mentions her husband: "Now Deborah, a prophetess, the wife of Lapidoth, was judging Israel at that time." Presumably Deborah's husband, Lapidoth, strongly believed in her calling and anointing, for he allowed her to go into battle with Israel's army with only the strength of the Lord's word to her.

Deborah certainly had discussed the plans with her husband and arranged for the household before her departure. In her political position, she most likely had servants to keep her house clean, her family's meals cooked, and household supplies purchased. However, she still fulfilled her obligation to her family. We can assume that she fulfilled her responsibilities at home before heading to the north, with her husband's consent, to war for Israel.

The Family: Our Greatest Testimony

Many women put great emphasis on the calling of God at the expense of their families. As wives and mothers, our first ministry is always to our families. We need to schedule everything around our family's needs.

We can't afford to forsake the needs of our families in pursuit of ministry. God's proper order never changes: God first, family second, ministry third. Reversing these priorities will cost us more than we could ever afford.

Our greatest victory and testimony is our family. We must continually ensure that our homes are in order before pursuing ministry. The same God who called us is also big enough to keep our families. And He does this with our cooperation, which we show by valuing our families with our time and attention.

So many women risk everything—even their families—in pursuit of their ministry. We need to realize something: Our ministry is not equal to our relationship with God! Knowing Him is much more important than serving Him.

As a single mom, I cooked my son's meals ahead of time, helped him complete his science projects, and attended teachers' conferences before I ever fulfilled any ministry obligation. I made sure that all of the necessary details in my son's life were taken care of before I departed to minister in any foreign country.

Likewise, Deborah ministered to her family before pursuing the mission God had placed before her. Then, in one day, Deborah went from wife, mother, and judge to soldier. And her first battle was with the notorious army of Sisera.

Without prior military training, she stood beside Commander Barak leading ten thousand soldiers. She didn't need army fatigues or military weaponry; her confidence was in the spoken promise of

God: "...against you I will deploy Sisera, the commander of Jabin's army, with his chariots and his multitude at the River Kishon; and I will deliver him into your hand" (Judg. 4:7 NKJV).

Just as He had said, God positioned Commander Sisera and his men for defeat at the hands of the army of Israel.

The Enemy's Seeming Advantage

The successful Commander Sisera knew that Israel's army was not as sophisticated as his own. He was secure that he was well advanced in weaponry and skill. When a nomadic herdsman named Heber informed him of Barak's strategies, he was prepared to swiftly defeat him.

> Now Heber the Kenite, of the children of Hobab the father-in-law of Moses, had separated himself from the Kenites and pitched his tent near the terebinth tree at Zaanaim, which is beside Kedesh. And they reported to Sisera that Barak the son of Abinoam had gone up to Mount Tabor.
>
> So Sisera gathered together all his chariots, nine hundred chariots of iron, and all the people who were with him, from Harosheth Hagoyim to the River Kishon.
>
> Judges 4:11-13 NKJV

Sisera may have known everything in order to advance to victory. But what he was not privy to was the Israelite's greatest weapon, Deborah—the woman willing to risk everything in obedience to God. He did not know of her spiritual discernment or her intimate relationship with God. In short, Sisera had no idea what he was in for!

Right when the enemy thought he had God's children where he wanted them, God was working a hidden strategy. Sisera was sure that he had Israel in his grip, and he defiantly took a step ahead of them—right into the battlefield where his army would meet its demise!

What he didn't know was that before he had ever touched his first weapon, God had been orchestrating a strategy to deliver His children and defeat the enemy. Sisera would soon have to come and bow down to the God of creation, the Maker of heaven and earth. The One who was, and is, and is to come was about to show Sisera who was Lord. The Lord God, strong and mighty in battle, had given Israel the victory before they even headed to Mount Tabor.

When Divine Timing and Purpose Intersect

The army of Israel knew that the Lord had given His oath to deliver the enemy into their hand. Exactly how and when He would accomplish this was yet to be known.

When God has purposed a divine plan, its fulfillment is contingent upon divine timing. The right thing at the wrong time equals disaster, and a missed opportunity is a failed opportunity. The Hebrew word for divine timing is *moed*. It is first introduced to us in Genesis 1:14 (NKJV), which says, "Then God said, 'Let there be lights in the firmament of the heavens to divide the day from the night; and let them be for signs and seasons, and for days and years.'"

Prior to this, there was no separation between time and eternity. Time had never been codified. The Alpha and Omega Himself, the only One who had the capacity and authority to do so, extracted time out of eternity.

When divine timing and purpose intersect, a miracle takes place. And Israel would soon see this principle in action as they acted on the Lord's orders given to Deborah.

Preparing for Battle

God spoke to Deborah, and she obeyed His voice. His divine orders were to attack Sisera's army on the appointed day and at the appointed time. He had gone ahead to set up everything that pertained to Israel's victory. Deborah's successful record in hearing and executing the plan of God had already validated her counsel, and, without any reservation, Barak moved out on her instructions from the Lord, which we find in Judges 4:14 (NKJV):

> *"Up! For this is the day in which the LORD has delivered Sisera into your hand. Has not the LORD gone out before you?..."*

Barak and his ten thousand men were convinced by Deborah's words that the Lord would execute His sovereign plan. This army of Israel was not experienced in war. None had been trained for battle. But it didn't matter that they were ill equipped in comparison to Sisera's army or that they had no horses to match Sisera's cavalry.

Ancient Bible historians teach us that Israel was inferior in iron technology until the years of David's reign. Their neighboring enemies, the Philistines, were masters of iron. However, God wanted Israel's trust to be not in the strength of weapons, but in the name of the Lord.

Military strategists explain that the reason the Israelites were not to war on chariots was that the battle took place on the flatlands bordering the Kishon River. In order to reach this place of battle, chariots would have to be disassembled and then reassembled. When God commissioned Deborah, He spoke to the elements and commanded rain to fall vehemently on the assigned day. This would put Sisera's chariot-driven army at a disadvantage.

Sisera's Army Met God's Opposition

Sisera never factored in the weather, much less a severe thunderstorm that would weigh down the chariots and cause them to become helpless in the midst of the storm. The clouds surrounded the enemy in ambush. As the clouds closed in on them and obstructed their view, flooding rains poured down upon them like missiles. The intensity of the downpour grew increasingly stronger until the flat plain was a flood of quicksand-like mud. The chariots began to sink into the huge suction hole, which pulled them down into utter defeat.

> ...*So Barak went down from Mount Tabor with ten thousand men following him. And the Lord routed Sisera and all his chariots and all his army with the edge of the sword before Barak; and Sisera alighted from his chariot and fled away on foot. But Barak pursued the chariots and the army as far as Harosheth Hagoyim, and all the army of Sisera fell by the edge of the sword; not a man was left.*

Judges 4:14-16 NKJV

Now, entrapped in an ocean of mud, the foot soldiers of Sisera's army plunged in for a clobbering defeat. There was no place to run to and nowhere to hide! The storm flooded the river, leaving the boastful army no way of escape. Lightning flashed across the sky and was followed by a deep chilling wind that led Sisera's aimless army into the swords of Barak and his men.

Extremely bewildered, Sisera's army was now a defeated foe. Once again God had revealed His master plan by delivering His people by His own outstretched arm. But a woman, a spiritual warrior for God, had led this defeat. She was a model of two dynamic attributes: modesty and confidence.

15

GOD KEEPS HIS WORD

Just when it looked as if God had truly outdone Himself, just when Israel was so ecstatic about their victory, Sisera escaped. Before plunging to their inevitable death, the army managed to secure Sisera's safety. The job was not quite finished yet.

You see, God would not allow Deborah's words to fall to the ground. She was not only a judge, but also a prophetess of God. He backed Deborah's words with surety. Sisera ran right into the lure that Deborah had prophesied: "Nevertheless there will be no glory for you in the journey you are taking, for the LORD will sell Sisera into the hand of a woman" (Judg. 4:9 NKJV).

Fleeing for his life, Sisera attempted to take refuge in a place he believed would ensure his survival. Little did he know that the Most High God had once again gone before His people into battle.

However, Sisera had fled away on foot to the tent of Jael, the wife of Heber the Kenite; for there was peace between Jabin king of Hazor and the house of Heber the Kenite.

Judges 4:17 NKJV

Out of all of the places to hide, Sisera ran to the camp of Heber, the nomadic tattletale who had originally told him of Barak's plans. Thinking Heber would empathize with him, he lodged there.

Jael's Strategy

Heber's wife, Jael, stood in the doorway of the tent. Just as Sisera breathed a sigh of relief in his newfound safety, she lured him into her tent.

> *And Jael went out to meet Sisera, and said to him, "Turn aside, my lord, turn aside to me; do not fear." And when he had turned aside with her into the tent, she covered him with a blanket.*
>
> Judges 4:18 NKJV

Sisera was confident that he was safe in Jael's keeping and had escaped destruction. He felt he had found a place of refuge where no one would find him. Who would expect a military man to take refuge in the tent of a woman? It was not customary for a woman to allow a man to enter her domain unless permitted by her husband, father, or brother.

However, Jael was not just any woman. Jael was indeed a warrior for God.

Thirsty from the battle, Sisera asked Jael for a drink. Jael didn't give him water but offered him milk.

> *Then he said to her, "Please give me a little water to drink, for I am thirsty." So she opened a jug of milk, gave him a drink, and covered him.*
>
> Judges 4:19 NKJV

Perhaps she slightly heated the milk, as a mother would do to help a baby relax and sleep. Then she covered him with a blanket, seemingly affirming her hospitality.

Then Sisera made these orders:

> *"Stand at the door of the tent, and if any man comes and inquires of you, and says, 'Is there any man here?' you shall say, 'No.'"*

Judges 4:20 NKJV

And at Jael's affirmation, Sisera slowly began to drift off into a deep sleep.

It was time for the word of the Lord to be fulfilled. He had promised to lead the enemy into their hands. If Sisera were permitted to live, he would raise up another army with fierce wrath against Israel and would not rest until they were destroyed.

Using what was familiar to her, Jael prepared to defeat the enemy. Her tribesmen were nomadic, and her job along with the other women was to pitch and dismantle tents. Over the years her arms had waxed strong as she had repeatedly performed these duties.

> *Then Jael, Heber's wife, took a tent peg and took a hammer in her hand, and went softly to him and drove the peg into his temple, and it went down into the ground; for he was fast asleep and weary. So he died.*

Judges 4:21 NKJV

Jael eased over to Sisera and drove the shepherd's stake into his temples, from one side to the other. Before he could ever rise again, he was plunged to his death. She literally nailed him to the ground!

Barak Saw the Fulfillment of Deborah's Word

In Barak's search for Sisera, he came upon the camp. Jael welcomed him.

And then, as Barak pursued Sisera, Jael came out to meet him, and said to him, "Come, I will show you the man whom you seek." And when he went into her tent, there lay Sisera, dead with the peg in his temple.

Judges 4:22 NKJV

When Barak asked of Sisera, Jael politely led him to the place where he lay. Where had her risky act of loyalty come from? Who would have ever thought that God would begin His master plan with a prophetess and end it with a hospitable nomadic woman?

When Barak saw Sisera's pierced head and lifeless body, he knew that indeed he had done the right thing in following Deborah's instructions. Just as Deborah had prophesied, God had given Israel their victory. The Lord did not allow one word to fail.

Ultimately, Israel completely defeated their oppressor, the king of Canaan.

So on that day God subdued Jabin king of Canaan in the presence of the children of Israel. And the hand of the children of Israel grew stronger and stronger against Jabin king of Canaan, until they had destroyed Jabin king of Canaan.

Judges 4:23,24 NKJV

Barak and Deborah Rejoiced Together

Then Barak beckoned Deborah to his side, and they rejoiced and sang together.

"...In the days of Jael, the highways were deserted, and the travelers walked along the byways. Village life ceased, it ceased in Israel, until I, Deborah, arose, arose a mother in Israel....

My heart is with the rulers of Israel who offered themselves willingly with the people. Bless the LORD!"

Judges 5:6,7,9 NKJV

"Most blessed among women is Jael, the wife of Heber the Kenite; blessed is she among women in tents. He asked for water, she gave milk; she brought out cream in a lordly bowl. She stretched her hand to the tent peg, her right hand to the workmen's hammer; she pounded Sisera, she pierced his head, she split and struck through his temple. At her feet he sank, he fell, he lay still; at her feet he sank, he fell; where he sank, there he fell dead."

Judges 5:24-27 NKJV

As a wise woman, Deborah never competed to seize all of the glory. She had an assignment, and this mission was completed. Deborah then wisely returned to her place of assignment as the mother of Israel and prophet to her people and remained to complete her assignment, a big part of which was serving her husband at home.

Many women in our society today are in positions more socially or economically prominent than their husbands. It would be so easy for a woman in this position to become prideful and to see herself lifted above the headship anointing of her husband. However, while it is wonderful to be assertive and confident, we must not take a place of dominance over our husbands. Instead, we need to balance our strengths and weaknesses with our husband's strengths and weaknesses. Then each spouse will be sharpened and become a lethal weapon not against each other but against the enemy.

The Blessing of a Supportive Husband

Deborah's husband is never spotlighted in the Scriptures, yet we can infer that he was a man of confidence and security because he flowed with Deborah in her calling and allowed her to go to battle. The Scriptures never reveal Lapidoth contending against Deborah or saying anything at all. Yet his silence speaks volumes of his character.

If your husband does not contend with what God has called you to do, you should bless the Lord at all times! But if your husband fights against what God has called him and you to do, prayer is a powerful tool.

Take a Humble Approach

Let me take a brief moment to address an issue that is vital to the success of your ministry and marriage. I have seen countless women fighting against their husbands for what they know God has called them to do. Some have even given their husbands an ultimatum: "Either allow me to answer the call, or I will divorce you."

If you have said that or thought about saying it, I want you to pump your brakes, take a deep breath, and exhale. There is more that one approach to most matters in life. Humility is an approach that will always turn away wrath.

May I suggest one very effective approach to your very complex challenge? First, never allow your husband to feel that he is second to your ministry. Your ministry and personal relationship with God are two totally different things. God is to be second to none. Your ministry is your service and offering to your Lord, and

your first ministry is to your family. The greatest ministry testimony that any woman can have is the testimony of her entire
household loving the Lord.

God is not anxious for anything; neither should we be.
Philippians 4:4-6 NKJV tells us:

> Rejoice in the Lord always. Again I will say, rejoice! Let your
> gentleness be known to all men. The Lord is at hand. Be anxious
> for nothing, but in everything by prayer and supplication, with
> thanksgiving, let your requests be made known to God.

If your calling is indeed of God, it will not expire. The God who
spoke to you so clearly is also able to speak to your husband. Let
your husband know that you appreciate him. Do not compare him
to your friend's husband who allows her the freedom to minister.
He must know that you love him more than your ministry. Go back
to your marriage vows: You made a covenant of ministry to your
husband that takes precedence over any outside ministry.

God's Word Is the Final Authority

If you married a man who promised to love and support you in
everything but seemingly became another man, keep your eye
focused on what God has said and not your husband's angered
utterances. God's Word is the final authority.

If your husband says, "I want a divorce!" you must think to
yourself, *Did God say this?* If he says, "I don't love you anymore!"
you must ask yourself, *Did God say this?* A dear, long-time friend of
mine once called me sobbing, saying, "My husband told me he
doesn't love me anymore and wants a divorce."

I exclaimed, "So what! Don't listen to his words! You had better listen to God's words!"

The Bible says, "There are many plans in a man's heart, nevertheless the Lord's counsel—that will stand" (Prov. 19:21 NKJV).

I told my friend, "While the words were coming out of your husband's mouth, a voice was coming to you from heaven." (See Daniel 4:31.)

At that moment all she could focus on was what her husband said. I had to disengage her from his words and challenge her not to agree with them.

I asked her, "Do you still love him?"

She said, "Yes!"

I asked her, "Do you want your man?"

She said, "Yes!"

"Then stop crying, and get ready to fight!"

If there is trouble in your marriage, your first assignment is to disregard every fear- or failure-driven word that comes out of your husband's mouth.

If God has called you to minister, the enemy will launch his attack against your family. In actuality, marriage is ministry. If your husband thinks you love the ministry more than you love him, your marriage is in danger.

By contrast, your husband will know he doesn't have to compete with your calling when you display a constant lifestyle of tender loving-kindness towards him. This will revitalize him and give God the open door to make a new man out of him.

Your greatest testimony is a house that is in order and flowing with the principles of God. Meet his needs, and let him know that he is a vital component for your success as a minister. Make him your ministry partner. Men are rescuers by nature, and they need to feel needed.

The same man who told my friend he wanted a divorce is now dating his wife again. Glory be to God! God has the final word, and divine order always comes before divine increase. Humility always comes before honor.[1]

Deborah's Humble Approach

Deborah's story exemplifies the rewards and honor that result from humility. Not only did she begin humbly, but she remained humble after her victory. She led Israel into a battle against one of the most feared armies of the day, but she didn't attempt to manipulate the situation for selfish political gain. She didn't see an opportunity to make herself marketable or to merchandise her strategy to other military strategists. Neither did she use the occasion of victory for her own platform of advancement or compete against Barak for the position of commander of the army.

Clearly, all of the army had seen Barak's need for Deborah by his side. She could have easily placed the limelight on herself. Instead of singing her own song, she joined Barak in praise of all those who had followed the Lord into victorious battle.[2]

Operating From Her Position of Strength

Then Deborah returned to her office as judge of Israel, the position where she was most needed and anointed. She knew God had called her to be the spiritual leader for her people, and she didn't need human accolades to boost her self-esteem.

A woman of strength is willing to be behind the scenes in order to advance someone else. In life sometimes we allow people to promote us beyond our divine assignment. We must stay in the vein of God's anointing and appointing. We are only gifted and anointed where we are called. The place of assignment is the place of power, provision, protection, peace, and purpose.

Deborah didn't try to pursue a military career. She had been in the army for the appointed assignment to lead her nation into victory. Barak had needed her to strengthen him, and he had trusted her enough to expose his weakness to her. She hadn't used this privileged trust to humiliate him, but instead she stood by his side to lead their people into united victory.

Even though Deborah was a woman of godly strength who possessed valuable traits of character, she yielded to the way of the Lord for her life. Though she was self-confident and assertive, she balanced those character traits with humility, modesty, and self-denial. Her wisdom mandated that she take the low road. She was unassuming and wise enough to avoid the glamour of the praise of people. She didn't allow the praise to contaminate her spirit, but she guarded her heart with all diligence, knowing it was the headquarters from which life's issues flow.[3]

Deborah's balance of humility coupled with obedience kept her stable, sober, focused, and pliable in the hands of the Master. This was why she was able to gain the victories she did and why she was able to continue to serve the Lord at home and in her ministry. Follow her example as an obedient and humble servant, and with the Word of the Lord, you will see your enemy defeated and God glorified every day of your life.

Prayer for Courage and Boldness

Lord, please help me to become bold in the areas of timidity in my life. I know that lack of boldness comes from fear and the failure to trust You in every given area of my life. You said that if I am in right standing with You I would be as bold as a lion. Please remind me daily that my confidence and hope lie in You because only through Christ Jesus I am able to do all things as You strengthen me in the undeveloped areas of my life.

Give me a courageous heart that is not afraid to do Your will. Lord, I desire to come to a place in my walk with You where purpose echoes louder than any residue of fear. I need You to show me, by the power of the Holy Spirit, the unidentified areas of fear operating in my life. Sometimes I am not even aware of hidden areas where fear is still housed. I want to walk in the perfect love that dispels all fear.

The more I am able to trust You, the more I find myself walking in boldness. I know that You are with me because Your rod and staff comfort me in the presence of my enemies. Your goodness and mercy are my rear guard and they follow me as long as I dwell in Your presence. Give me a solid revelation of You as the Greater One living inside of me. Help me to understand, and reveal Yourself as the omnipotent One who rules and reigns in my life! All might and power has been given unto me in Your name; therefore, in Your name I have dominion over the earth. By Your strength, I can run through a troop and leap over a wall.

My strong confidence is in the reverential fear of the Lord because it is in You that I move and live and have my being. Father, I practice my boldness when I come before Your throne to obtain mercy and find grace to help me in my time of need. I refuse to live a life of intimidation or a life of seeking man's approval or valida-tion. My hope is in You, Oh, Lord. You are making me into a vessel that is well pleasing unto You. I seek Your approval and I bind every spirit of control over my life because the Lord Jesus Christ is my Master and Lord!

You, Oh Lord, have not given me a spirit of fear, but of power and love and a sound mind. Therefore, I enter the Holy of Holies by the way of the blood of the Lamb. I am able to boldly say that the Lord is my helper and I will not fear what man can do unto me because You will never leave me or forsake me; You will be with me to the ends of the earth.

Scriptures

Proverbs 14:26, 28:1; Ephesians 3:21; Hebrews 4:16; 10:19; 1 John 2:28; 4:17; Ephesians 6:10.

Daily Declaration

Today I put on the whole armor of God so that I am able to stand against the wiles of the enemy. I do not take my armor for granted because my Master provided it for me and I am instructed to be strong in the Lord and in the power of His might. My battle is not with flesh and blood, but rather against principalities, powers, and rulers of darkness in this age. I war against the spiritual host of wickedness in heavenly places; therefore, I put on the full armor of God so that when the day of evil comes, I may be able to stand my ground, and after I have done everything, to stand. Stand firm then, with the belt of truth buckled around my waist, with the breastplate of righteousness in place, and with my feet fitted with the readiness that comes from the gospel of peace. In addition to all of this, I will take up the shield of faith, with which I can extinguish all the flaming arrows of the evil one. I will take the helmet of salvation and the sword of the Spirit, which is the Word of God. I will pray in the Spirit on all occasions with all kinds of prayers and request. With this in mind, I will be alert and always keep on praying for all the saints.

PART 7

~~~~~

RAHAB:
"NOT WITHOUT MY FAMILY"

16

A GENTILE PROSTITUTE MEETS GOD

Rahab was a prostitute born outside of the covenant, yet she was completely convinced that the God of the children of Israel was a faithful God. God had a master plan for Rahab that demonstrated her value to Him far beyond the value men placed on her as a prostitute. This woman soberly entrusted her entire life to a God whom she had never seen and with whom she had never acquainted herself. Her undaunted faith reached God's attention, and He rewarded her for her faith by giving her a part in maneuvering His children into their inheritance.

Rahab's story comes near the end of the biblical account of the Israelites' journey to the Promised Land. The generation that had been freed from slavery in Egypt was almost completely gone now, and Joshua led this present generation in the final phase of their journey to the Promised Land.

The only obstacles separating them from their destination now were the Jordan River and the fortified city of Jericho. There always seems to be that final obstacle on the way to the promised land. The final quest always seems to be the most trying. There is always that last giant to slay, river to cross, or wall to scale. God had not brought the children of Israel this far to allow them to fail, and He has not brought us this far to allow us to fail! He had drawn them this far to bring them into their inheritance, but they would never enter in without first confronting Jericho.

Indeed, a promised new life awaited them, but it would not be theirs without a fight. The people of Israel at this time were used to warfare. News of their victories in battle had spread throughout the land. Not only had God defeated their foes in battle, but He had daily fed them from heaven.[1] They had never needed to sweat for provision. This was the only type of life many of them had ever experienced.

However, the manna would not continue to simply appear for them forever. Their clothes would no longer last them their whole lives. Their soft, unworked hands would soon have to learn to use the plow and shovel to produce grains and to slaughter cows to attain clothing and meat. The people of Israel would have to work hard to claim and maintain their promised life.

A Final Observation

Positioned on the border of the Jordan River just across from Jericho, the people of Israel were anxious to cross over the Jordan, pass through Jericho, and attain their promise. However, Joshua ordered a final observation of the city pitched between them and the land God had given them. As the people of Israel made the final preparations to move into their new territory, Joshua commissioned two spies to go into Jericho and bring back an accurate report.

*Now Joshua the son of Nun sent out two men from Acacia Grove
to spy secretly, saying, "Go, view the land, especially Jericho...."*

Joshua 2:1 NKJV

Five days would come and go before the scouts returned. It was harvest season in the land, and it was indeed harvest time for the children of Israel. After wandering forty years, anticipating the occupation of their new land, their reward and their harvest awaited them. The season was Abib, when the snow melts from the Lebanon mountains and causes the banks of the Jordan to overflow.

Safe Lodging in Jericho

The Israelite spies entered Jericho incognito, not wanting anyone to identify them as men of Israel. Knowing they would have to find lodging, they carefully weighed their decision about where they would stay. There were many inns in this prestigious city, but where would be the safest place to lodge? Finally, the two spies decided to stay in the home of Rahab.

In Eastern culture, a man would never be permitted to stay in the home of a woman without clearance. However, God had arranged this scenario by design. The circumstances and standards were different in this situation because Rahab was a prostitute. The authorities never monitored the activity of the harlot's house because it was customary to see strange men go in and come out.

Rahab's home would prove to be very helpful to them also because it was atop the wall of the city. It was the perfect location from which to survey Jericho. The two spies studied carefully the entryway into the city, the width of the walls, the strongest pillars, and the fortified gates. Here, they could observe everything necessary to make a proper evaluation to deliver to Joshua.

Concealing the Spies

As soon as the spies entered her home and told her of their assignment, she hid them on her roof. Soon afterward, a knock came at her door, and she was greeted by servants of the king, demanding that she bring out any men who had entered that day. Joshua 2:2-3 NKJV explains:

> And it was told the king of Jericho, saying, "Behold, men have come here tonight from the children of Israel to search out the country." So the king of Jericho sent to Rahab, saying, "Bring out the men who have come to you, who have entered your house, for they have come to search out all the country."

Someone had told the king of Jericho that Hebrew spies were within the city gates. Rahab was wise enough not to dispute their coming to the king, but to still protect the men, saying:

> "...Yes, the men came to me, but I did not know where they were from. And it happened as the gate was being shut, when it was dark, that the men went out. Where the men went I do not know; pursue them quickly, for you may overtake them." (But she had brought them up to the roof and hidden them with the stalks of flax, which she had laid in order on the roof.) Then the men pursued them by the road to the Jordan, to the fords. And as soon as those who pursued them had gone out, they shut the gate."
>
> Joshua 2:4-7 NKJV

Suddenly, Rahab found herself placing her life on the line for two men she had just met. Rahab had to think quickly as she directed the men towards a false location of the spies. If discovered, she would be found guilty of treason and executed.

The soldiers left in pursuit of the spies, and Rahab shut the door.

Speaking to the Spies

Rahab tiptoed upstairs to where she had hidden the spies and informed them of the news of the city. She was risking so much at this point that confiding in these two men was naturally the next step. She knew that Jericho was doomed to utter destruction at the hands of the Israelites' God, so it was time to negotiate with the men whose God she had come to believe. Speaking to the spies, she said:

> *"I know that the LORD has given you the land, that the terror of you has fallen on us, and that all the inhabitants of the land are fainthearted because of you. For we have heard how the LORD dried up the water of the Red Sea for you when you came out of Egypt, and what you did to the two kings of the Amorites who were on the other side of the Jordan, Sihon and Og, whom you utterly destroyed. And as soon as we heard these things, our hearts melted; neither did there remain any more courage in anyone because of you, for the LORD your God, He is God in heaven above and on earth beneath."*
>
> Joshua 2:9-11 NKJV

Rahab was by no means naive! She knew exactly who the spies were and why they had come. She had heard the news in Jericho of how the God of Israel had fought for them from the time they exited Egypt until that day.

God had allowed the news of the Israelites' previous victories to precede them and, as a result, fear had gripped the hearts of the people of Jericho. They knew that the Lord had dried up the Red Sea for the children of Israel. Surely it had been the talk of the town long before the spies had come to scout out the land. The more the people of Jericho talked about the victories of the children of Israel, the more they were magnified in their eyes. They had also heard about the Israelites' victory over their neighboring Amorite kings, Sihon and Og.

God had caused the testimony of the children of Israel to melt the hearts of the men of Jericho to the point that there was no courage left within them. This report from Rahab was more valuable than the spies' own surveillance. Because of this, the spies knew that the people of Jericho were weakened already. Both men knew the importance of being strong and courageous because this was the first command that the Lord had given Joshua after the death of Moses.[2] They already had the word of the Lord assuring them that no man would be able to stand against them all the days of their lives.

Rahab Made Her Request

Rahab knew how to gain the ear of men of great stature, and she wanted to make sure to talk to the spies before they returned to their camp. She had opened her negotiation with the statement "I know your God has given you the land." Now she would tell them her desire:

> "Now therefore, I beg you, swear to me by the LORD, since I have shown you kindness, that you also will show kindness to my father's house, and give me a true token, and spare my father, my

mother, my brothers, my sisters, and all that they have, and deliver our lives from death."

Joshua 2:12,13 NKJV

In order to take the city, the children of Israel had to destroy the wall upon which Rahab's home was built. Rahab knew that the destruction of the wall would mean losing everything she had worked for, all of her life's possessions. Her only hope was to barter for her life and the lives of her entire household.

She would have to trust the spies, and the spies would have to trust her. But who would trust a harlot's words? She had made the first move by jeopardizing her life to hide them. But how could she dream of asking these two children of God to spare her life—the life of a prostitute? She had no covenant, no Hebraic inheritance, and no worthy profession. She desperately needed mercy.

Rahab Needed Mercy

Psalm 9:18 says, *"For the needy shall not always be forgotten: the expectation of the poor shall not perish for ever."* Rahab was poor in her soul and desperate for change, and God would not forget her or leave her to perish.

Two of the most powerful attributes of the Master are His willingness to forgive and His patience. These two qualities give humanity space for repentance. His love, His provision, His guidance, His power, His omnipotence, and all of the qualities of His nature exalt Him as the Most High God. Psalm 113:4-5 (NKJV) tells us:

The LORD is high above all nations, His glory above the heavens. Who is like the LORD our God, who dwells on high?

He elevates the rejected and forsaken to seat them with royalty.

He raises the poor out of the dust, and lifts the needy out of the ash heap, that He may seat him with princes—with the princes of His people.

Psalm 113:7,8 NKJV

God remembers the needy when everyone else forgets them. The needy are not always the poor. Some of the neediest people are those in exalted positions who are empty inside. Rahab's home was high upon the wall of Jericho, but she had a deep need.

The Master's mercy extended the arms of forgiveness to Rahab, and His mercy provides for us salvation. His truth establishes His will, and His mercy intercedes for us especially when we don't deserve it. His mercy is unmerited, unearned, and undeserved. God's everlasting mercy will compel us to find Him. Even when we have stumbled into the deepest pit, His outstretched arms will be there to keep us from falling. His mercy crosses boundaries and cultural borders and doesn't have to be authorized by anyone but Him. "To You, O Lord, belongs mercy; for You render to each one according to his work" (Ps. 62:12 NKJV).

The Lord shows mercy on whomever He chooses,[3] and once He does it is a settled issue. For Rahab, His mercy was only awaiting her request.

17

A REQUEST FOR A COVENANT

Rahab didn't have a long time to make her request. The Scriptures portray her as a woman of few words who knew how get to the point. She assessed the situation, and the required response was obvious. The reputation of Jehovah was sure: Without mercy, she and her family were destined for a quick death among the people of Jericho—unless she could convince the spies to repay her for her kindness.

Once they left her house, it would be too late to ponder what she should have done. The time of opportunity was present. There was no time for procrastination, intimidation, or timidity. She had to come boldly before the only two men with the power to divert the imminent death of her family.

Rahab knew that Asarte, the god of her people, was unable to help her. Rahab had faith only in the God who was faithful to His own people, and as a result the Father moved upon the spies' hearts as she pleaded with them to spare not only her family but also their possessions.

Rahab held her breath, waiting for the spies to respond. When they did, the mercy of God was evident. His orders had been to go in and possess the land, and in times past He had instructed them to utterly destroy everything. However, this time a woman's act of faith pleased Him and grabbed His attention.

"Our Lives for Yours"

The men responded, "Our lives for yours."

> *So the men answered her, "Our lives for yours, if none of you tell this business of ours. And it shall be, when the LORD has given us the land, that we will deal kindly and truly with you."*

Joshua 2:14 NKJV

Knowing she could have immediately run out to tell the king of their plot to take the city, the men made the covenant exchange: Their lives for hers. They were taking just as much of a risk on her as she was on them, so they made the agreement.

The Conditions of the Covenant

Though the spies told Hagar that she and her family would be spared, they also told her that their protection would come only if she convinced her family to never utter one word of these events. If one family member broke the promise and revealed the secret, then the covenant would be broken and the deal would be off.

In life, we are responsible to follow the terms of the covenant. People sometimes blame God for the consequences of their own disobedience. They might accuse God of not answering their prayers, when in actuality they violated the conditions to the covenant. Deuteronomy 28 spells out the requirements for the blessing and the curses for disobedience. God doesn't make His covenant requirements a mystery. He purposefully clarifies His will in the Bible.

He said He places before us the choice of life and death, and then He encourages us to choose life.[1] We get to choose what God has already chosen for us. He alone knows the right path, the journey that has been navigated by His will.

Life is filled with choices that can either lead us into the Lord's will or on a path of self-will. When we don't know which choice to make, we have a divine compass within to direct us. God said that if we would only trust in Him with all of our heart and continually lean not to our own understanding but on Him, He would direct our path.[2] If we involve, acknowledge, and invite Him in our lives, He promises to guide our footsteps on His path for our lives.

God never intended us to move out alone on an endless journey of doubt, aimlessly following fate. His "yes" is "yes," and His "no" is "no." There is no gray area with God. He doesn't obscure Himself to His people. He makes the rules and ways of His kingdom crystal clear for us.

When the Master Decrees "Yes"

The Master's "yes" is all the confidence we need to move out, sight unseen. We can rest assured that no matter how difficult the task may appear, God will never leave or forsake His own.[3] When the Master has decreed "yes," the manifestation of our request will appear. When the Master says "yes," we must do just what He says.

A confident word from God becomes our weapon in warfare. We turn to God in different times in our lives and ask Him to say "yes," but we have already proven that we know how to make a mess of our lives without Him.

However, if God is not in it, neither should we be. Live in the vein of obedience. Follow when the Master says "yes." Flee from the path to which God has said no! It doesn't matter how much you want something, you have to trust that God knows what you need more than you could ever imagine. As you yield to God, He will give you a heart to do His will.

That is when you can pray the prayer of consecration: "Not my will, but Your will be done." Never press for what God has not approved. If God has said no, then no amount of sacrifice will alter what He has decreed. Don't waste your time trying to change God and manipulate Him to grant your desires. True fulfillment only comes when God says "yes." We only find peace in the place where God says "yes."

A journey other than the one God has approved for you will take you far from His intended will for your life. If you don't know what move to make, wait and make your choice sure. If you ask God for direction and open your heart to His design, then He will speak to you.

We can't tell God how to orchestrate our lives. He is the author of life and the developer of our faith.[4] He desires to be there with open arms to welcome us into the path that He has chosen for us. He will never force us onto His path. Neither will He delay letting us know if we are headed the wrong way, for delays are too costly to our destiny. He does not take pleasure in complicating life's choices, but in prospering us.[5]

However, even with God's "yes," there will be challenges. But we will always triumph in Christ Jesus when the Master says "yes."

Our Father's promise to His people is that the blessings that He has in store for us will not be postponed.[6] The blessings have been commanded to overtake us as we obey His voice.[7] The curses of disobedience are just as real as the blessings, but as long as we follow God's command we will eat of the good of the land.[8] Our protection is in obedience.

Entering a Covenant With God

Likewise, Rahab's protection was in her obedience to the terms of the covenant. Here was a Gentile woman, a prostitute, entering a covenant with the chosen people of God! Knowing little about the God of Israel, Rahab asked for a "true token" of their intentions. Without realizing it, she was tapping into the heart of God. God is a covenant-keeping God who keeps His promises and covenants for every generation. He says, "My covenant I will not break, nor alter the word that has gone out of My lips" (Ps. 89:34 NKJV). Once He says it, it is so.

Rahab didn't realize that she never needed to identify the token she asked for as a "true" one because God only deals truly. He cannot lie. There is no room for falsehood in Him. Psalm 119:160 (NKJV) says, "The entirety of Your word is truth, and every one of Your righteous judgments endures forever." Truth is automatically encompassed in God's promises.

In a demonstration of God's mercy and the power of the covenant, Rahab and her entire Gentile family were given the opportunity to align themselves with the children of God. Rahab and her family were about to receive and benefit from everything that the children of Israel had taken forty years to possess!

The Scriptures tell us that without faith it is impossible to please God.⁹ In one act of faith, Rahab pleased God! Now He would give her and her family the milk and the honey of the Promise Land, even though they had so recently served a foreign god.

When God had instituted the covenant with His people, Rahab's people were sacrificing to Asarte, who demanded endless sacrifices. They would no longer have to make a sacrifice for their crops, another for their health, and another for their protection. The God of the children of Israel was strong and mighty enough to feed, protect, clothe, shelter, and watch over His people. And His care demanded not sacrifices but obedience. His care came as the result of His tender loving-kindness.

Rahab must have thought, *I like this God.* She and her family were about to become regal refugees among His people—because of His mercy and because she dared to ask.

18

A HOUSE OF MERCY AND REDEMPTION

When it was time for the spies to leave Rahab's house, she boldly spoke and acted in faith, as though she were already redeemed.

> Then she let them down by a rope through the window, for her house was on the city wall; she dwelt on the wall. And she said to them, "Get to the mountain, lest the pursuers meet you. Hide there three days, until the pursuers have returned. Afterward you may go your way."
>
> Joshua 2:15,16 NKJV

Here were two generals—proven to be valiant men of war, part of the company that had defeated the kings on the other side of the Jordan—taking the advice of this woman. In their response, they even spoke to her as if she were in charge.

> So the men said to her: "We will be blameless of this oath of yours which you have made us swear, unless, when we come into the land, you bind this line of scarlet cord in the window through which you let us down, and unless you bring your father, your mother, your brothers, and all your father's household to your own home. So it shall be that whoever goes outside the doors of your house into the street, his blood shall be on his own head, and we will be guiltless.

And whoever is with you in the house, his blood shall be on our
head if a hand is laid on him. And if you tell this business of ours,
then we will be free from your oath which you made us swear."

Joshua 2:17-20 NKJV

Twice, in verse 17 and verse 20, the men said Rahab had made
them swear to her oath. Of course, she could not have made them
do anything. Rather, they were following the will of God, for she
had found favor with Him.

Remain in the House

The conditions to the covenant were not only that she and her
family be silent about the pact, but also that every family member
be in her house at the time of the attack.

The spies made the oath not with her parents or relatives but
with only Rahab. Through these two men, God treated Rahab as
one entitled to the covenant. The Messiah, in whose human pater-
nal ancestry she would ultimately be, was not yet born; but even
now, before the planned time for redemption, His compassion to all
people began to reach out.

The two spies spelled out the details with specificity. As long as
she tied a red cord in the window, and as long as she and her family
remained in the house, they would be spared.

God teaches us a powerful lesson from this scene in the life of
Rahab. As long as she remained in the house, she was protected.
Likewise, as long as we remain in obedience and in fellowship with
God, we are covered by His protection. The Bible says, "Those who

are planted in the house of the LORD shall flourish in the courts of our God" (Ps. 92:13 NKJV).

The men pledged their lives to protect Rahab's family as long as they were in the house. Many of the covenant blessings we receive can only be distributed "in the house." Get planted, get active, be faithful, and remain committed "in the house"—in other words, in a local church. Once they wandered outside of the house, the oath would be violated.

These are the conditions of the covenant: We must do it God's way in order to get God's result. There is no way around it. As women desiring to be used of God, we must solidify this principle in our thinking. God obligates Himself to His own agenda. He is sure that He will perform the words of His own mouth without delay, according to Ezekiel 12:28.

If we obey the terms of the covenant, then we will benefit from its promises. As long as we walk uprightly before the Lord, He will never withhold any good thing from us.[1]

There is another powerful message in this scenario from Rahab's life. God took a house that was once a house of ill repute and made it a covenant house of blessings and protection. Likewise, because of the covenant God made with humanity through Jesus, He can turn a person of ill repute into His holy temple.[2] What a demonstration of the covenant we find in Rahab's story!

Putting Action to Her Faith

After hearing the spies' promise, Rahab had all the security she needed to proceed in faith and action. Her last words exemplify the trust she had in the covenant: "According to your words, so be it" (Josh. 2:21 NKJV). Then she put action to her faith: "And she sent them away, and they departed. And she bound the scarlet cord in the window."

If only we would trust God at the level that Rahab trusted His children to honor their word! God's Word is all we need to depend on in order to see the manifestation of His promise. Rahab didn't ask for a written contract, oil from Egypt, or water from the Red Sea; rather, at their word she believed and acted on her belief.

Likewise, all we need is one word from God. God credits faith as righteousness.[3] Our belief in Him, our taking Him at His Word, pleases Him.[4] We should place more confidence in God's oaths and promises than in anything else in the world. It's His promise—not prayer cloths, anointing oil, or water from the Jordan—that will not return void.[5] Our faith should be rooted and grounded in God's Word.

When God looked at Rahab, He saw a woman who would bank everything she owned on a word from the Lord. He saw a woman who governed her life by oaths. He saw a woman of great faith. Ultimately, He saw a woman fit to carry on the lineage that would lead to the Messiah.[6]

The Task of Convincing Her Family

Rahab was a woman of her word, and she believed God would rescue her and her family because of the word of His children. However, how would she convince her entire family to abandon their gods to trust in the God of the two spies?

We can see that she indeed believed that He was the Most High God. She had said to the spies, "...for the LORD your God, He is God in heaven above and on earth beneath" (Josh. 2:11 NKJV). However, she couldn't introduce Him as her own God.

Her father and mother only knew of sacrificing to appease Asante, whom Rahab knew to be a lifeless god who couldn't hear, see, or touch. Rahab had to convince not only her parents, but also her brothers, who would have to convince their wives. She also had to convince her sisters, perhaps who had not chosen the profession of Rahab.

It is debatable whether Rahab was a temple prostitute or a commercial prostitute. Either way, she slept with men as a means of exchange. How could she convince her family to listen to her when she had made this apparently inferior career choice?

Even more, how could she expect them to believe that the God of the spies was the Most High?

Much hung in the balance. Rahab's ability to convince her family of the truth would determine whether her family would live or die. If any one of them had sent word to the king of the family's association with the spies, every one of them would have been found guilty of treason and executed.

After convincing them to stay with her, Rahab also encouraged them to bring their possessions under her roof. Her family members might have had much bigger estates than hers, but the promised protection would only be found in her house.

Rahab's word alone convinced them to act. She was trusting in the spies' word, and the spies were trusting in her word. All these lives were on the line, and the only collateral was the salt of each one's word.

The Spies' Safe Return to the Camp

Rahab had given the men the instruction to wait three days in hiding in the mountains before continuing to their people. She had even told them exactly where to hide. Knowing precisely where the spies were, Rahab could have easily betrayed them and turned them in to the authorities of Jericho, but she didn't.

The three spies safely returned to the Israelites' camp, thanks to the loyalty and trust of Rahab. Joshua 2:23-24 NKJV describes the scene when the spies returned to the Israelites' camp:

So the two men returned, descended from the mountain, and crossed over; and they came to Joshua the son of Nun, and told him all that had befallen them. And they said to Joshua, "Truly the LORD has delivered all the land into our hands, for indeed all the inhabitants of the country are fainthearted because of us."

Upon their return, Joshua sought the Lord for His battle plan, and the Lord told him:

"See! I have given Jericho into your hand, its king, and the mighty men of valor. You shall march around the city, all you men of war; you shall go all around the city once. This you shall do six days. And seven priests shall bear seven trumpets of rams' horns before the ark. But the seventh day you shall march around the city seven times, and the priests shall blow the trumpets."

Joshua 6:2-4 NKJV

Waiting in Jericho

The people of Jericho knew Israel was about to make its move on the city, and their fear had driven them into hiding within the gates. Verse 1 describes the scene in Jericho during this time: "Now Jericho was securely shut up because of the children of Israel; none went out, and none came in."

Rahab knew the days of peace in Jericho were coming to a close. One by one her family members had joined her in her home to await their promised salvation. It had been challenging enough just to get them all together. Once there, though, she had to be sure that they did not go out for anything.

A Strange War Tactic

Finally the day came for the children of Israel to begin their march around the city, as God had instructed them. From her home atop the city wall, Rahab could see them surrounding the city, but she couldn't hear them speaking a word. In unity, they marched around the city wall without weapons.

Rahab must have been thinking, *What kind of war strategy is this?* Her brothers could also see the Israelites from her house on the wall. "What are they doing, Rahab?" they must have asked. But there was no way she could describe their tactics. It was not her job to understand; it was her job to trust and obey God.

Likewise, when we can't figure God out, when we can't trace Him or track Him, we should simply trust Him. However, this is not always easy.

The pressure must have mounted in Rahab's house. Parents, brothers, sisters, in-laws all remained under one roof. The sisters-in-law had to submit to the instructions of their husbands, following Rahab's oath from an unknown God. The brothers-in-law had to listen to their wives as they all followed Rahab's plan of deliverance. If anyone revolted and refused to remain under the roof, the oath with that person would be canceled. The blood of that person would be on his or her own head.

The March Continued

The next day, day two, the children of Israel began their second silent march around the city wall, again without weapons. Even when their feet got tired, they did not open their mouths to complain. One wrong attitude could have blown the whole attack.

When day three arrived, as the sun rose over the Jordan and as Rahab and her family peeped out of the window, nothing had changed. There were the children of Israel silently marching again. Everyone in the city must have been discussing this strange phenomenon.

On day four, Rahab's family must have been suspicious of the whole plan she had given them. The sisters- and brothers-in-law must have wondered what on earth they were doing there. If Rahab's words were true, then they would never see their loved ones again. The pressure was mounting to run back to their families.

By day five, even the father was probably questioning their decision. He was too old to defend them or produce another life for them. His daughter had convinced the entire family of hopes for a better life. The only problem was that he didn't know enough about their future to tell them anything, except that he knew the reputation of the God of Israel—that He kept His word.

There weren't many options for Rahab's family at this point. They could either come into agreement with the oath that she had convinced them to make, or they could blow the entire deal and run toward the temple to offer a sacrifice to Asante. After five days, they had come too far to turn back.

On day six, the entire family must have started to wonder about the Israelites' tactics. Maybe some of them thought, *How long do these crazy people plan to march around the city?* Then their thoughts turned to a serious matter: "Do we have enough food in the house to provide for every person?"

Only a Word and a Reputation

Rahab's family might have asked, "What day will they strike, Rahab?" She had no answer; the only thing she knew was the word that the spies had given her and the reputation of the Hebrew God.

Finally, day seven came. Rahab's family had nowhere to go. They were settled into the plan now. Surely, as time ticked by, Rahab asked herself, "Am I making the right decision?" But Rahab had to trust in the "yes" of God.

Rahab risked everything she had for the Master's "yes"! Just before the daily doubt could take its grip and garrison around the family's intellect, the house began to tremble and they heard the great unified shout of the children of Israel. Like an earthquake, a war was brought about by words—by the Israelites' shout of praise.

Every single brick on the wall crumbled except the foundation that housed Rahab's home. There at the gate of the city mounted high above the debris and shambles of ruins was the house of Rahab, just as secure as it had been the day it had been built.

Not one of the family members was harmed. Once again God had been faithful to His word. The family lived to appreciate Rahab and to see the fulfillment of the word of the God of Israel. There was no Jericho city now; the land was now in Israel's possession. Each member of Rahab's family had the opportunity to live amongst the children of Israel and to become recipients of the land flowing with milk and honey.

Because of Rahab's faith, she and her family became partakers of the divine covenant. Not only that, but perhaps the greatest lesson in Rahab's story is that God so valued her faith in Him that He ultimately used her to continue the bloodline that would lead to the Messiah.[7]

Mercy Has Found You

It didn't matter to God that Rahab was a prostitute. What mattered to Him was her faith, and His mercy reached out to her. Even if no one had believed Rahab could be delivered and used of God, mercy did. Rahab believed that the Lord God Almighty would deliver His people, and mercy found her.

Today, mercy has found you. It's the mercy of God that has intervened and kept you alive until this day. You may have looked death in the face, but mercy said, "Not so, not now, not here! I won't allow you to have her! I know she deserves it—she's guilty, she has sinned—but you cannot have her!"

Like Rahab, we have done nothing to deserve God's mercy. We know our weaknesses and can remember the former entrapments of sin. But mercy showed up in our most desperate moments and made a way of escape. Mercy became the sacrifice that saved us from our penalty.

Mercy selected Rahab, a Gentile harlot, and broke the grip of the sin of her profession. Mercy saw what no other person could see and gave her a second chance at life. She had no other hope but mercy.

The Light of Mercy

Once mercy embraces us, it will never let us go. While others mock and judge us, mercy will defend and promote us. Mercy allows us to become who God intended us to be. Our past can never dictate our future, no matter how bad it was. The light of mercy will dispel the darkest trace of sin.

When our past rises to haunt us, mercy steps in to say, "She is redeemed! She is righteous!" Our redemption and righteousness are not based on our own sacrifice, but simply upon God's mercy toward us. Mercy frees us to dream and begin again. Mercy positions us in righteousness, and when our Father sees us, He sees us through the blood of Jesus. Because mercy intervened for our lives, we will never have a cloud over us but only an open heaven.

When there was nothing left in us that seemed valuable enough to salvage, mercy continually interceded for us. The accusations and persecutions of man can never win against mercy once we have been embraced by it. Nothing in your past or in your future could win against mercy.

Receive every act of redemption, and walk in your righteousness. You have been justified. When someone brings up your past, remind yourself that mercy has redeemed you. You are a new creature; old things are passed away; all things have become new.[8] Walk in all the blessings and freedom that cost the Father God the blood of Jesus.

You have been washed by the blood of the Lamb. Anyone who judges you stands in judgment of God. Mercy has already judged you and remitted your sins. Every weakness is under the blood and woe to anyone who would tamper with what has been placed under the blood. That's why it is the seat of mercy, the place where God meets His people in the tabernacle.

You are free from guilt, shame, and your deepest hidden reproach. Guilt can no longer confront you for that act that no one knows about but you. You are already forgiven, and no abortion, adulterous act, or prison term can hinder where you are going in God. Mercy has come to intercede for you this very day!

Prayer for Faith in God's Word

Father God, I thank You for wrapping Your nature up in the bound pages of the Bible. Awaken my understanding and help me to remember the truth of Your counsel. Your Word is forever settled in heaven, and all of earth will pass away before one letter of Your Word will fail. It's not always so easy for me to remember that Your Word is just as faithful as You are; You and Your Word are one and there shall never be any separation between You and Your sovereign Word.

For me to have faith in You, I must have faith in Your Word because this is one of the most primary ways You have chosen to talk to me. It is more sure to me than prophecy. Your Word is the weapon You have given me to daily defeat the enemy. Your Word is a divine compass to my feet and it lightens the path to my prophetic journey in life. You are a constant in my life and You are faithful to lead me into each season of my life.

Father, the entrance of Your Word brings illumination and understanding to the complex issues of my life. Your Word cleanses me and calms my fears; therefore, I choose to anchor in the Word of the Lord. My faith is in Your Word continually, and I will meditate in it day and night. Help me to keep my mind stayed on Your Word so that I can possess the peace I need to remain sober when life's stresses compel me to waver.

I need You, Father, and I am not ashamed to acknowledge my need and dependency upon You and Your Word. Your promise to me, my Lord, is that if Your Word abides in me and I in You, then I can ask whatsoever I will and it shall be done unto me. You promised me that You would do this so that You may be glorified.

Be pleased with my prayer, Oh Lord, be pleased with my worship, and be pleased with my desire to do Your will and my hunger to make Your Word the final authority in my life. I receive Your Word as my daily bread because man can only live by every

Word that proceeds out of the mouth of God. I hide Your Word in my heart, and I believe that for every challenge and opposition that I face, I must bow to the counsel of Your majestic Word. When I am tempted to take matters into my own hands, help me to stand upon the Word of God! Help me not to be moved by what I see, but to trust in Your Word because Your Word is what upholds the entire earth.

How simple of me to doubt Your Word when it is powerful enough to frame the world and noble enough to be exalted above Your majestic name. I need You, Lord, to give me a greater measure of revelation into Your Word and help me to bring every thought into obedience to Your Word, even when my present circumstances may look totally diabolical to the promises of Your Word.

Father, You are beyond words and I stand in awe of Your goodness that You continually bestow upon me. When I am in need to be encouraged, I find comfort in the counsel of Your Word. I will always make my decisions based on Your Word. It is my schoolmaster in life and my divine guide as I journey in the path of Your predetermined course for me.

Scriptures

Psalm 119:24,42,50,165,116; 1 Corinthians 13:2,13; 2 Corinthians 1:24; 5:7; Galatians 2:16; 3:11; Ephesians 3:12; 4:5; Colossians 1:23; 1 Thessalonians 1:3; 2 Thessalonians 3:2; 1 Timothy 1:19; 5:8.

Daily Declaration

I confess today that I purpose to make the Word of God my priority. I hide the Word of God in my heart continually so that I will not live a lifestyle of striving against God. Your Word declares that I will have great peace as I develop a love for Your Word. I proclaim that Your Word sustains me. I will stand upon Your Word and hold on to it until the end of time. The Word of God is shaping and molding my character daily. Your Word is producing life in me and my supreme counselor in life is the Word of God. I have good understanding of the Word of God because the Holy Spirit is my teacher. The Word of God is germinating in me, and I place my total trust in the integrity of God and His Holy Word. It is the final authority in my life.

PART 8

ESTHER:
"IF I PERISH"

19

GOD'S HIDDEN GEM

It is God's design to hide His own until their appointed season of unveiling. Such is the case with Esther, a hidden gem whom He jealously preserved, protected, sheltered, and veiled until the appointed time of unveiling.

Throughout history such hidden gems have proven not to be seekers of notoriety, power, human acceptance or applause. Seemingly obscure, they are the Master's lethal agents assigned to covert operations. They are instructed to seek the face of the King much more than the audience of humanity.

Just as precious gems are found in the low things of the earth, God's hidden gems are formed and refined in sometimes painful obscurity. Yet they find satisfaction in yielding to the Master's plan. They pass through life's disappointments and the brutal oppression of opinions, yet they allow no bitterness to mar their beauty.

The Lord decides when to unveil and exhibit His hidden gems. They never have to seek their own exhibition. It is His show, and His hidden gems are vessels of His glory. This is the most powerful lesson we can learn from the life of Esther.

Hidden in Persia

Esther 2:6 explains that Esther and her cousin Mordecai were in Persia because their people had been carried away from Jerusalem by Nebuchadnezzar the king of Babylon.

Esther's birth name was Hadassah, which means myrtle. The myrtle is a common plant that is easily overlooked and plain—until its leaves are crushed and bruised. Once the leaves are bruised and crushed, they give forth an appealing and sweet fragrance.

In this imagery, we can begin to see the untold story of Esther's life. The crushed and bruised areas of Esther's life were the hardships of growing up without a father and a mother.[1] Life can either make us bitter or better, but it is obvious that throughout Esther's life she chose the latter. She allowed the crushing to make her sweet and graceful.

Esther's life demonstrates a life of self-denial. With every stage of preparation, she died to her own ambitions until death no longer threatened her. She learned to submit to and trust the wisdom of Mordecai, her cousin, who had taken her as his own daughter when her parents had died.[2] Without any stretch of the imagination, we can see that life was no bed of roses for this adopted girl.

A life without a mother and father is enough to challenge and scar any child for life. However, it is apparent that Esther learned very much through the things that she suffered. Likewise, many generations later, our Redeemer Jesus would learn obedience through the things that He suffered.[3]

Concealed in the Shadows

The Talmud reveals that Hadassah used her Persian name, Esther, to conceal her Jewish identity. She was not allowed to reveal her true essence but, for a season, had to mask her identity. The pun on the Persian name *Hesther* means concealment. Esther willingly became concealed and hidden within the shadows, awaiting the Master's bidding to come forth. This time of training prepared her for the divine assignment awaiting her.[4]

Little did she know that the fate of the entire nation was contingent on her willingness to yield during these preparatory years. We may never know the struggles she faced during this season of concealment, fighting against her true self and the metamorphosis she would have to undergo before she nestled into her ultimate divine purpose.

Esther had years of foundation laying in her life. Her season of being crushed and the working of a contrite heart would prepare her for the palace. The character development in the hidden seasons of her life prepared her to maintain the stature of humility when the season of exaltation embraced her.

Grooming Her Inner Beauty

The beauty of Esther was groomed in the secret place of her heart. Her inner beauty preparation was the formative stage of preparations for her divine purpose. In the New Testament, Peter opens our eyes to a secret: "Do not let your adornment be merely outward…," he says, "rather let it be the hidden person of the heart, with the incorruptible beauty of a gentle and quiet spirit, which is very precious in the sight of God" (1 Peter 3:3,4 NKJV).

Today, one of the most lucrative industries in the world is cosmetics. Sadly, many women place their value on the external perceptions of beauty when what really matters is the beauty of the heart.

Esther was a woman with a beautiful heart, and it took her places even she could not have imagined. Esther had the hand of God upon her life from the beginning and was arrayed with favor from on high.

Favor With God and Man

When Persia's King Ahasuerus called for the most beautiful virgins in all of his provinces to come into his quarters, Esther was taken to his palace. Placed under the care of Hegai, the king's custodian of the women, Esther found favor in his sight. A man accustomed to working with the most beautiful women in the land, Hegai noted something radiant about Esther. As if he knew her destiny, Hegai allotted Esther extra portions of beauty preparations beyond the designated allotments for the other women.

Furthermore, Hegai assigned choice maidservants to Esther from the king's palace. Surrounded by favor from heaven in her preparatory season, Esther flourished while learning the customary ways of diplomacy of the palace.

Just as her body was anointed daily with expensive ointments, Esther's favor perpetually worked for her. For example, Hegai relocated her to the best and most secluded place in the house.

A Season of Separation

Esther had not asked to be moved but had unquestioningly yielded to Hegai's orders. When God begins to prepare us, He will first separate us from the crowd and uproot us from the normal ways of our lives. We must learn how to interpret this season of our lives. It is not a season of rejection but of separation, sanctification, and consecration. We see this pattern repeated throughout history in the lives of those whom God chose to impact the world. In addition to Esther, such people as Abraham, Joseph, Moses, and Daniel went through a time of separation before their purpose was unveiled.

God separated Abraham from his family and social upbringing. He disconnected Joseph from his culture and family, and his classroom of consecration began in a pit provided by his own brothers. Moses' bachelor's degree in separation came from the backside of a desert, and he received a his master's degree in persecution and prayer from the very people he gave his life to deliver. Daniel's place of consecration and separation began in his prayer closet and continued in a lion's den.

When it is our season of separation, we must stop trying to escape, trying to squeeze into another spot where we do not fit in. Our seasons of getting alone with God, severing relationships, and pulling away are just as vital to our assignment as our response to His calling.

During this time the Master uproots mindsets, paradigms, opinions, habits, hang-ups, fears, and frailties. As we seek Him continually, we are changed in the presence of a holy and loving God. In this season, God doesn't want the interference of our personal agendas or others' to push us off of His predestined path for our lives.

We have to stop expecting everyone to understand that God is moving in us. It's not for all to understand, because it is an inward working. We must stop trying to take our friends in the prayer closet with us, because this season is designed for us individually and God alone!

Don't be so surprised when you are no longer invited to lunch or called to the annual gatherings. It is not rejection; it is God's method of separating you. Though you may feel lonely, you alone are being groomed for your purpose.

All of the other candidates in King Ahasuerus' courts were groomed and trained to wear the crown, but it was Esther alone whom God preserved, observed, and deposited the necessary traits and attributes in for this divine assignment.

Esther kept her mouth closed in her season of separation and, according to Mordecai's instructions, concealed her identity.[5]

A Season of Preparation

As Esther remained secluded from the public, Mordecai made it his practice to check on her every day.[6] According to the regulations for the virgins called into the king's palace, Esther's season of separation lasted twelve months. There was no allowance for a plea of expediting the process; each woman simply had to endure her preparations: six months of myrrh and six months of perfumes.[7]

One of my mentors in ministry, the late Daisy Osborn, taught me that time spent in preparation is never lost time. God will use everything in our lives that we've gone through and weave the wealth of knowledge we have extracted from our life experiences to make a beautiful tapestry of His workmanship.

This is why it is important not to misinterpret the season of preparation. For every student, every waiting homemaker, and every corporate woman desiring the next promotion, Esther's story demonstrates the key to the success of your patient endurance: Keep your eyes upon the Lord!

When God has us in a holding pattern, there is always a reason. Though we do not always understand His reasoning, we must trust in His perfection. He is a perfect God; it is absolutely impossible for Him to make a mistake or fail.

We must remind ourselves that the same God who strategically ordered the steps of our lives into a path of righteousness is the God who will fulfill our most earnest expectation.

We cannot see what the Master sees. We see in part.[8] Our Father reveals to us His secrets on a need-to-know basis. However, one sure way to qualify for the revealing of His mysteries is to fear Him, as Psalm 25:14 (NKJV) says: *"The secret of the LORD is with those who fear Him, and He will show them His covenant."* As we seek to do God's will and thirst for the depth of His sovereign desire to be our own, He will prepare us for the path He has charted ahead.

God always gives us everything we need to do what He commands. His way of equipping us begins before we are ever aware of His workings. Psalm 33:15 declares that the Lord fashions our hearts individually and considers all our works. He has specifically fashioned and equipped you for your life's journey. It was the unique assignment God had for you that determined your fashioning.

He prepares and equips us on an individual basis, and He will judge each one on an individual basis. In 2 Corinthians 5:10, Paul reveals that each one of us will be judged based on our individual deeds, works, and assignments.

Our seasons of preparation are not to be taken lightly or used as a time to plead and negotiate with God to expedite the process. We can just save our breath, because He won't! The foundation of a building determines its towering height. The greater and deeper the foundation, the higher the building can rise.

20

A YIELDED VESSEL

When it was time for Esther to meet with the king, while the other women chose their own favorite apparel for their royal meetings, Esther wisely and gracefully bowed to the advice of Hegai. Hegai had learned from the reign of Vashti that the worst thing a queenly candidate could display before the king was a self-willed life. After all, Queen Vashti had lost her royal position for abusing her privileges and falling into radical rebellion.

Hegai knew exactly what the king was looking for and he could see in Esther's eyes that specific grace and the poise of a yielded vessel. Like the constant agitation and friction of the oyster that yields the precious pearl, life's disappointments had formed Esther's contrite spirit. Season upon season of preparation eventually produced a life displaying the glory of her Master. Ripened, tried, proven, and anointed with the fragrance of obedience, she was now prepared for the Lord's purpose and pleasure.

In Luke 22:42 we see our Lord demonstrating this yielded desire in the Garden of Gethsemane, His place of separation and consecration. With great turmoil, self-willed desires competing harshly and intensely against God's will and desire, our Lord bowed gracefully and yielded to the desire of His Father and responded, "Not my will, but thine be done."

Likewise, Esther had learned to yield. She didn't resist authority but, rather, found safety in accountability. Deprived of her parents at a young age, she had learned to find refuge and safety in the counsel and authority of her cousin and adoptive father, Mordecai.

Esther had learned to practice a life of discretion. The Scripture says, "As a ring of gold in a swine's snout, so is a lovely woman who lacks discretion" (Prov. 11:22 NKJV). The other women in the king's palace may have been lovely, but Esther had the radiant gift of discretion distinguishing her from the rest.

God had appointed Esther for this assignment. Finally, after twelve months of preparations, it was Esther's time to meet the king, and she was ready to walk in her place of purpose. She had passed the test of separation and preparation. Her desires were not her own, and her meat was to do the will of Him who had placed her, an orphan girl, in the royal palace of Persia.[1]

Before the King

The appointed time for Esther's meeting with the king was the tenth month, Tebeth, in the seventh year of the king's reign. The number seven is the number of completion,[2] and King Ahasuerus was about to be completed with Esther by his side.[3] When Esther was taken to the king, both Hegai and Mordecai must have been eager to hear good news. Without a doubt, Mordecai had been praying for his cousin to find favor in the sight of the king.

The moment King Ahasuerus laid eyes on Esther, each one of the other candidates became a fading shadow in the light of the glory encompassing her. She instantly captured his favor and grace as she confidently strolled into his midst. The nearer she approached the throne, the more his heart yearned for her. His desire was stimulated beyond sight and by a deep sense of knowing that she was the one.

Esther never needed to contend, compete, or compromise to gain the king's favor. God had appointed and anointed her for this particular position at this set time. One of the constant realities of God is that what He has for *you* is for *you!* No other person can wear your crown, and no other person could wear Esther's crown or fulfill her purpose.

21

THE DIVINE UNVEILING

Soon it was time for Esther to take her rightful place as the new queen of Persia. As King Ahasuerus placed the royal crown upon her head, Esther's efforts were crowned with success. Simultaneously, the Master crowned Esther's year with goodness and her predestined path dripped with regal abundance. (Ps. 65:11.)

God used Esther to temper an irate king. She made her way into his heart with her graceful presence, but she would also one day capture his confidence with her wise counsel.

The reputation of Esther's new husband wasn't completely flawless. She was very much aware of the fact that he had sent away his previous wife simply because she had embarrassed him with one rebellious act.[1] Esther's husband seemed to be a man with unsettled issues in his life and a man who indeed ruled with a strong arm. Only at his invitation could anyone be allowed in his presence, and he was quick to execute judgment on anyone who defied his orders.

The marriage between this Gentile king and this Jewish orphan likely was not easy, but Esther's gentle and quiet spirit chiseled away every wall that the king had constructed around his heart over the years. Esther obtained his favor, the greatest thing that would be required in her reign as queen of Persia.

A Murderous Plot Exposed

One day, her cousin Mordecai uncovered a plot against King Ahasuerus. One of the king's eunuchs told Mordecai that Bigham and Teresh, royal doorkeepers, were plotting to murder him.

Mordecai informed Esther, who wisely warned her husband and also reported her source. After confirming the story, King Ahasuerus immediately had the two plotting men hanged in gallows. The information was credited to Mordecai when the account was archived in the book of the chronicles of the king.[2]

The King's Mad Counselor, Haman

Esther's new position came with more than just glamour and privileges. It came with an unbelievable amount of responsibility. God needed an uncompromising woman at King Ahasuerus' side to intercede for His people.

At King Ahasuerus' side also stood the mad, power-seeking, egotistical, Jew-hating counselor, Haman. After the plot against the king was revealed, Haman's seat was elevated above all of the other princes of the region. All of the king's servants bowed to Haman.[3]

Mordecai, a man of principle who had trained Esther to be a woman of principle, refused to bow and pay homage to Haman. This infuriated Haman, who planned to show Mordecai no mercy. When the king's servants questioned Mordecai about his open protest, he revealed his Jewish identity. The servants rushed to inform Haman, who was determined to destroy not only Mordecai but his entire race.[4]

Esther had now been queen for five years, and Haman launched his all-out attack against Mordecai and her people. Haman told the king about these certain people scattered and dispersed among his territory in all the provinces. With the king's swift and unadvised support, Haman wrote a decree for the day of holocaust for the Jews.[5]

Mordecai's Cry

When Mordecai heard the news of the impending slaughter of his people, he tore his clothes and cried out with a loud voice in the center of the city.[6] Mordecai's heart and mind were in turmoil for his people.

When Esther's maids brought her news that Mordecai was in sackcloth before the palace doors, she quickly sent proper clothes to him. But he refused to accept them. Then she sent one of the king's eunuchs to Mordecai to learn what was the matter, and Mordecai explained the impending danger and sent her a copy of the decree. He also sent word to Esther to ask her to go before the king and plead for her people.[7]

The moment of truth confronted Esther; she faced the very hour of her purpose.

Esther's Fearful Response

Everything that Esther had been prepared for through the years now awaited her action, but her initial response to Mordecai was one of fear:

"All the king's servants and the people of the king's provinces know that any man or woman who goes into the inner court to the king, who has not been called, he has but one law: put all to death, except the one to whom the king holds out the golden scepter, that he may live. Yet I myself have not been called to go in to the king these thirty days."

Esther 4:11 NKJV

Esther hid behind legalism from the responsibility that lay before her. However, her words reached Mordecai in a place that gave him a completely different perspective. Outside the seeming safety of the gates with the rest of his people, Mordecai could see that even Esther was not safe in the palace. His words came with weights of conviction to Esther.

"...Do not think in your heart that you will escape in the king's palace any more than all the other Jews. For if you remain completely silent at this time, relief and deliverance will arise for the Jews from another place, but you and your father's house will perish. Yet who knows whether you have come to the kingdom for such a time as this?"

Esther 4:13,14 NKJV

As Mordecai's words reached Esther's ears, they pierced her heart. Mordecai brought her focus back to her purpose. She was not safe just because she was in the palace. She was a Jew and no safer than any other Jew in the kingdom. This was a wake-up call for Esther.

Called to Purpose

Mordecai's words reminded Esther who she was, where she had come from, and most importantly, what her purpose was. Mordecai awakened her to the responsibility attached to her privileged position. Yes, she was the queen, but she belonged to God and He had given her life and positioned her to deliver His people.

All that we have and everything that we are only by the grace and design of God. Every promotion, every increase, and every degree we have received has been obtained by the help of the Almighty. He is the very air that we breathe, our life, and the length of our days.[8]

Mordecai made her understand that if she wouldn't allow God to use her to deliver His people, then He would raise up someone else to deliver them. No matter what Esther decided to do, God would never forsake His own. But this was her opportunity to save not only herself and her family, but all of her fellow Jews living in Persia.

"If I Perish, I Perish"

Esther could not keep silent any longer. It was time to speak for those who had no voice. With no longer pause, she replied with conviction:

> "Go, gather all the Jews who are present in Shushan, and fast for me; neither eat nor drink for three days, night or day. My maids and I will fast likewise. And so I will go to the king, which is against the law; and if I perish, I perish!"
>
> Esther 4:16 NKJV

Esther now understood why she was in the palace: God had placed her there for this very moment. Her concluding statement to Mordecai illustrates her newfound identification with her people.

She didn't say, "If you perish...." She said, "If I perish." She had died to self and reached a new peak of obedience to God in order to save His people. She was willing to be obedient even to the point of death.[9]

Esther had come to a place where she reckoned herself dead to everything except what God had called her to do. Her story exemplifies the crucified life that the apostle Paul teaches us about in Galatians 2:20 NKJV:

> I have been crucified with Christ; it is no longer I who live, but Christ lives in me; and the life which I now live in the flesh I live by faith in the Son of God, who loved me and gave Himself for me.

Esther's position now had new meaning, and it was time for her identity to be exposed—even if it ultimately meant her death.

Esther's Strategy

Preparing to put her life on the line, Esther groomed herself to appeal to the king's eye. It had been thirty days since she had last seen him.

Esther clothed herself in her very best and prepared her countenance so that she was pleasing to him. This is exactly what happens to every one of us as we come boldly to the throne of grace to obtain favor and mercy in the sight of our Lord. Esther's fingers were on the pulse of God. When we please the king, He grants us our hearts' desires.[10] There is absolutely nothing that the king will withhold from us when we walk uprightly before him.[11]

Clothed in her royal robe, Esther stood in the doorway in the inner court until the king saw her standing there. Her presence once again captured him, and immediately he favored her and extended his scepter to grant her entrance. As Esther touched the top of the scepter, the king promised to give her whatever she desired—up to half the kingdom.

Esther's Invitation

An unwise woman could have taken this opportunity selfishly, but Esther considered not her own gain but only the deliverance of her people. However, Esther did not rush into her request. Instead, she invited the king and Haman to a banquet in their honor. The king quickly responded and ordered Haman to do as Esther requested.

Haman was flattered at the invitation to dinner with the king and queen. God was a step ahead of the enemy, and he played into His very hand.

At the banquet, Esther served the two men wine. Then, when King Ahasuerus offered Esther her desire—up to half the kingdom— she responded with an another invitation to a banquet the next day. Though she was apparently simply buying time, Haman was ecstatic.

As he left the banquet, Haman was brimming full of pride and happiness—until he passed the king's gate and Mordecai once again refused to bow to him. Haman stifled his anger for the moment and went home to boast to his wife and friends of his newfound accomplishments.

However, one concern robbed Haman of his full pleasure— Mordecai's refusal to bow to him. So he and his family devised a plan to get rid of this annoyance.

God Worked on Mordecai's Behalf

Mordecai was not aware of Haman's plan to murder him, but while he slept at the king's gate, the Lord began to work on his behalf. That night the king could not sleep, so he ordered that the book of the records of the chronicles be read to him.

As he listened, he heard the record of Mordecai's saving his life by exposing a plot to kill him five years before. Five is the number of grace, and God was about to extend grace to Mordecai through the king. When the king asked what honor had been bestowed upon Mordecai for his act of valiant loyalty, his servants replied, "Nothing."

At that moment, Haman entered to discuss with King Ahasuerus the troubling issue of Mordecai and his own proposal to hang him in the gallows in the morning. So conceited and insolent was Haman that his own pursuits were all he could see. When King Ahasuerus asked Haman what he should do for someone he wished to honor, Haman assumed he intended to honor him! Therefore, thinking he was organizing his own celebration, Haman said:

> "For the man whom the king delights to honor, let a royal robe be brought which the king has worn, and a horse on which the king has ridden, which has a royal crest placed on its head. Then let this robe and horse be delivered to the hand of one of the king's most noble princes, that he may array the man whom the king delights to honor. Then parade him on horseback through the city square, and proclaim before him: 'Thus shall it be done to the man whom the king delights to honor!'"
>
> Esther 6:7-9 NKJV

Immediately, King Ahasuerus sent Haman to do just as he had said for the man the king wished to honor—Haman's greatest source of frustration, Mordecai himself! Haman was humiliated, leading the kingly robed Mordecai on horseback around the town. When Haman told his counselors and his wife of everything that had happened to him, they responded with this solemn warning:

> "...If Mordecai, before whom you have begun to fall, is of Jewish descent, you will not prevail against him but will surely fall before him."
>
> Esther 6:13 NKJV

No weapon formed against Mordecai would prosper. Every scheme of Haman against Mordecai would lead to his own demise.

Esther's Identity Revealed

While pondering his wise men's counsel, Haman was rushed to Queen Esther's second banquet. With an anxious heart, Haman entered the room where the king and queen sat. Once again King Ahasuerus asked Esther to name her request. Now was the time to execute God's plan of vindication and deliverance for His people. Using this potent moment to honor God and not her own desires, Esther pleaded with the king to spare the life of herself and her people.

In that moment, Esther revealed her identity. There would be no more hiding, no more worrying what the consequences would be. She was past the point of no return. With deep conviction, she explained to the king the abusive oppression of her people:

> "For we have been sold, my people and I, to be destroyed, to be killed, and to be annihilated. Had we been sold as male and female slaves, I would have held my tongue, although the enemy could never compensate for the king's loss."
>
> Esther 7:4 NKJV

The Enemy Revealed

When Haman had requested the annihilation of the Jews, he had not told the king that the people were Jews. Furthermore, the king did not known that his wife was a Jew. Suddenly, King Ahasuerus was filled with rage: Who would presume to destroy the king's own wife and her people?

When he had voiced this question, Esther's gentle yet resolute response shocked him: "The adversary and enemy is this wicked Haman!" The king rose up in furious wrath, and Haman fell before Esther and pleaded for his life—but to no avail. When the king returned, he found an unthinkable scene: Haman was lying on the couch tugging on Esther's clothing. He was pleading for his life, but the king saw something altogether different and infuriating. "Will he also assault the queen while I am in the house?" he demanded.

And his words rang the death toll for Haman. As soon as he had said them, Haman's face was covered and he was carried to the gallows which he himself had built for his now-exalted enemy, Mordecai.

God's Reward for Esther's Obedience

God rewarded Esther's obedience beyond her wildest imagination, and she handed over her reward to the man who had cared for her all of her life. When she introduced Mordecai to King Ahasuerus as her relative, the king took off his signet ring and gave it to Mordecai. When the king gave her Haman's house and authority, she gave Mordecai that authority.

Though Haman was dead, Mordecai and Esther still needed to secure the protection of their people from a future slaughter Haman had scheduled. Once again, Esther went before the king and pleaded for her people's lives. The king held out his scepter to Esther and granted her the authority to make her own decree for her people.

Our King has granted each of us the authority to make a decree, and He backs us with His authority. He has destroyed our enemies and made a public display of their defeat.[12] We possess eternal protection because whatsoever we bind on earth is bound in heaven and whatever we loose on earth is loosed in heaven.[13]

We can ask whatever we desire and it will be given to us. Even more than half the kingdom, He will give us the ends of the earth for our inheritance![14] Our Father always hears our prayers. It is time to make your request known to Him today![15]

Esther's decree afforded the Jews the right to protect themselves, and they defeated all those in the land who sought their death. Mordecai was justly rewarded and Esther reigned as queen of Persia, free to live without hiding.

The most amazing point of this divine encounter is rarely told. Esther 8:17 says, "Then many of the people of the land became Jews, because fear of the Jews fell upon them." The enemy had been dethroned, and the Jews' jubilation provoked many to convert to Judaism so that they, too, could benefit from the covenant of peace. Is this not the finality of the story of the Gospel!

God delivered an entire nation by one woman who paid the price of obedience and radical faith in God. We can have this same attribute of obedience if we abide in Him and He abides in us.

The Unveiling of God's Hidden Gem

Esther's story demonstrates the totality of the heart of God—the faithfulness of God and the sovereignty of God. Where was Esther? She was found in the king's court because she far exceeded all the other candidates. Wherever she walked, she demonstrated the fact that her dynasty was divine destiny. Her neck was gracefully stretched because she had practiced looking up to the hills from which her help came.[16] She understood and accepted that she was a servant to her husband, the king. She was his favorite. He trusted in her counsel because her words were words of wisdom, with which she built her home.[17] Her tongue was the chief architect that shaped the imagery of her future.

Where was Esther? She patiently waited her turn and moved only when the king bade her to come. Her chaste and consecrated life preserved her reputation and testimony; the king knew that she belonged to him alone.

Where was Esther? A woman of principle, she firmly held on to her future. Refusing to compromise, she pressed toward her goal on behalf of her people. Though delicate and beautiful, she was like steel in the face of adversity. Death could not grip her, for she was a courier of truth and life. She was a deliverer for her people and an activist for justice.

Where was Esther? She pondered her words before she spoke and executed her strategies at the appropriate time. She did not rush anxiously in revenge but methodically waited for her plan to unfold.

Where was Esther? The maturity of her character harnessed her will when she was tempted to take the path of least resistance. She was anchored in fidelity and could not be lured to lower her standard. She empathized with the suffering of her people, though she was positioned in the palace. Her luxurious prosperity did not cloud her view or erase the memory of her humble beginning. She took a risk to not keep silent, to choose purpose over pleasure.

Where was Esther? She entered the presence of the King of kings before gracing the king of Persia with her presence. Esther had indeed counted the cost of obedience. She came before her king, her faith expecting the approval of his scepter, without which she would be put to death. The king beheld her after a season of separation, and the glory of her Father enveloped her flawless beauty and summoned the attention of the king. She chose her words carefully, and the king responded in her favor.

Where was Esther? She was the king's bride, she bore his name, and she had captured his heart. Her love for him came softly and slowly as she danced her way into his heart. The authoritative king who commanded irrevocable decrees had found himself smitten by the Almighty abiding in her person. She spoke on His behalf, and the king listened to her, for she stimulated him in a realm beyond the physical. He admired the courage she possessed to come behind Vashti, the former queen whom he banished for refusing his command.

Where was Esther? Esther, the hidden gem, stood in the gap for her people, and the Lord delivered them. She could have chosen to silently remain in the shadows. But the passionate thunder of her purpose echoed louder than the voice of compromise. Israel was vindicated, and a royal decree of protection for her people was archived. She returned to her place of assignment to wait patiently for the voice of her eternal King saying, "Well done, My daughter!"

Prayer for Self-Denial

Father God, the only way I will ever be able to master the attribute of self-denial is with Your help. I thank You that I have Jesus as my example who just happens to be my intercessor and advocate. There is no temptation known to man nor has there ever been except which is common to man. This lets me know that being a person of self-denial is attainable because other women have had to pass this same place of proving and testing in their lives. You are not testing me; the enemy is testing the Word of God in my life.

I know, Heavenly Father, that I will come through as pure gold because I am crucified with Christ and I set my affections on things above, because I am dead and my life is hidden with Christ in God. Only You can help me to esteem my fellowman higher than myself. I seek not my own, but rather I seek how I may help my brothers and sisters in Christ.

My life is not my own; I have been purchased by the blood of the Lamb. Help me not to think of myself more highly than I ought. Your Word shows me that if I trust in You I should rejoice and shout for joy because You are my defense. Help me to put my total trust in You, Father. I find myself in trouble when I try to take matters into my own hands. Help me to count all things as loss in exchange for the knowledge of You, Lord.

Father, help me not to look out for my own interest, but also for the interest of others. Holy Spirit, I call upon You now to convict me daily to put to death my members and to be willing to give of myself as an available vessel. I am Your workmanship created for good works.

Dear Lord, as selfish as I may be from time to time, I believe that I can walk in self-denial with the help of the Holy Spirit. Help me to see my self-interest as shadows in the light of Your will. Help me to go the extra mile and to turn the other cheek and give my all when someone is requesting my assistance. As unpleasant as it feels when I am going through this process of self-denial, I know that You are working Your character within me and I am being prepared for eternity; this character trait will be with me even into eternity. So I refuse to get off of the potter's wheel until the heat of Your purging fire removes the chaff from my life.

You are preparing me to be a vessel that can take things and not display ungodly behavior or character. In the areas that You need Your presence the most, send me. Help me to see continually that life is not about me or catered around me, and I do not seek to have my own way. I forfeit my compulsion to be right or first. Help me to find peace in taking the low road. Help me find fulfillment in esteeming my brother or sister higher than myself.

Show me myself, Lord, and reveal to me by Your Spirit the areas of my life that I have not surrendered to You. Help me to develop the fruit of love, joy, peace, patience, kindness, goodness, faithfulness, self-control, and gentleness. I need every fruit operative in my life so that I can be a vessel of honor that models the very essence of a woman of self-denial.

Father, it is not easy to live in an age that screams for liberation and views submission and self-denial as being weak. But I choose to be molded into the perfect image of Christ no matter what man thinks. Help me to commit to this daily until the full statue of my character is made manifest in my daily life.

Scriptures

Romans 14:1-22; 15:1-5; 1 Corinthians 6:12; 8:10-13; 9:12-27; 10:23; Galatians 2:20; Philippians 2:4; 3:7-9; Colossians 3:5; 2 Timothy 2:4; Revelation 12:11; Acts 2:24; Matthew 16:19.

Daily Declaration

I confess that I walk circumspectly before the Lord. I choose daily to seek opportunities to show and demonstrate to the world the love of God, which is shed abroad in my heart by the Holy Ghost. I reckon myself to be a dead woman walking. I purpose to mortify the deeds and the needs of my body. I decrease so that Christ can increase within me.

I will not seek after my own interest, but rather the interest of my fellow believers. Regardless of how hard my challenges may be or how resistant my flesh contends to have its way, I choose to deny myself for the sake of the Kingdom that is bigger and broader than I. My life affects the lives of others; therefore, I am a joint who is supplying to others and someone is depending on me to die to myself.

No longer will my self-willed determination rule over my spirit man. I count not my life dear to myself; I forsake all for the sake of Christ because if I love my life, I will only lose it. Help me to live a life that is pleasing to the One who enlisted me. I refuse to entangle myself with the impeding cares of this life. Daily I put off the old man and renew my mind to the ways of the Father. Christ the Anointed One and His anointing lives *big* within me today!

CONCLUSION:
POSITIONED FOR PURPOSE

My sister, I charge you to position yourself to accomplish the very thing that you were born to accomplish. You may need to take a deeper look at the work you have been doing. Even if it is a good work, it may not be a God work in this season of your life.

Exchange activity for purpose. Seek out the high calling, which the Master designed for you to fulfill before time began. (2 Tim. 1:9.) Pray that the eyes of your understanding may be enlightened so that you will begin to understand the path He has chosen for you, and that you will know He is bringing you to an expected end! (Eph. 1:18; Jer. 29:11).

Your challenges, disappointments, and seasons of waiting will be explained as you open up your heart to allow God to do His ultimate work in you.

God has a plan for you. The choice to live up to anyone else's expectations will cost you your holy calling, your eternal purpose, and the Master's gracious design for your life. My prayer is that the divine blueprint for your life will begin to unfold as you ponder what you have read in the previous pages and that, like the great women of faith depicted here, you will return to the original path that has been skillfully charted for you.

Taking a risk to fulfill the destiny God has for you will cost you something, but the risk is worth it. There isn't anything that you give up that God won't supply. God wants to bring you blessings beyond your wildest dreams.

Seek the hand of the Master. Yield to His gentle hand and allow every hidden reservoir of purpose, talent, and ability to spring forth and water every parched dream that you have been denied. Delay does not equal denial. Now is your season! You have been chosen for such a time as this!

Endnotes

Introduction
[1] 1 Peter 2:25 KJV.
[2] Romans 8:37 KJV.
[3] 2 Corinthians 2:14.
[4] Matthew 19:26.
[5] See 1 John 5:4.
[6] 1 Corinthians 10:13.
[7] Philippians 1:6 NKJV.
[8] See 2 Corinthians 5:7.
[9] Isaiah 55:9.
[10] See Ephesians 1:11 KJV and AMP.
[11] Hebrews 13:21 KJV; 2 Timothy 1:9; Ephesians 1:4.

Chapter 1
[1] Hebrews 6:13.
[2] Genesis 13:2,6.
[3] Genesis 12:2,3; 13:16; 22:17,18.
[4] See Genesis 16:3.
[5] See *Biblesoft's Jamieson, Fausset, and Brown Commentary,* electronic Database, copyright © 1997 by Biblesoft, all rights reserved, "Genesis 16:2…3."
[6] Genesis 16:4.
[7] *Biblesoft's Jamieson, Fausset, and Brown Commentary,* electronic Database, copyright © 1997 by Biblesoft, all rights reserved, "Genesis 16:1."
[8] James Strong, "Hebrew and Chaldee Dictionary" in *Strong's Exhaustive Concordance of the Bible* (Nashville: Abingdon, 1890), p. 114, entry #7793, same as #7791 from #7788, s.v. "Shur," in Genesis 16:7.
[9] Genesis 25:18 NKJV; 1 Samuel 15:7 NKJV.
[10] 1 Samuel 27:8 NKJV.
[11] John 17:3; Jeremiah 10:10; Psalm 89:6; Exodus 20:3.
[12] Philippians 2:13 NKJV.
[13] Romans 12:1.
[14] Strong, "Hebrew and Chaldee Dictionary," s.v. "contrite," Isa. 57:15, entry #1793 from #1792, p. 30, "crushed (literally powder…)."
[15] 1 Peter 5:6.
[16] William Smith, LL.D., *Smith's Bible Dictionary* (Old Tappan, NJ: Spire Books, Fleming H. Revell, May 1981 16th printing), s.v. "Kadesh, Kadesh-barnea," p. 320, "holy."
[17] Strong, "Hebrew and Chaldee Dictionary," s.v. "Kadesh," Genesis 16:14 entry #6946, the same as #6945, p. 102, "sanctuary."
[18] Strong, "Hebrew and Chaldee Dictionary," s.v. "Bered," Genesis 16:14 entry #1260 from #1258, p. 23, "hail."

[19] Hebrews 13:20,21 AMP; 2 Timothy 1:9.
[20] Hebrews 1:3 KJV, NIV.
[21] See Romans 8:28.
[22] See Isaiah 53:5.
[23] John 14:6.
[24] Galatians 3:7,16,22,26,29; Romans 11:17.
[25] See Colossians 2:8,9.
[26] See 2 Peter 1:3; Philippians 1:6; Hebrews 13:5; Psalm 46:1; Hebrews 4:16; 12:2 NIV; 2 Timothy 1:6; Luke 11:13; Philippians 4:19.

Chapter 2
[1] Galatians 5:22,23.
[2] James 4:8.
[3] Luke 22:42 NKJV.
[4] Luke 11:2 NKJV.
[5] Genesis 16:11 NKJV; see also v. 15.
[6] John 3:30.
[7] James 1:4.
[8] See 1 Chronicles 17:23.
[9] Matthew 24:35.
[10] Genesis 16:16.
[11] Genesis 17:1.
[12] Genesis 17:3-5.
[13] Genesis 17:19.
[14] Genesis 15:4 NKJV.
[15] Genesis 17:1,19.
[16] Genesis 18:10 NKJV.
[17] Genesis 21:11-14 NKJV.

Chapter 3
[1] Philippians 4:13.
[2] See Proverbs 31:27 NKJV; Psalm 1:2 NKJV; Galatians 3:24; Psalm 119:105.
[3] Joshua 1:8.
[4] Psalm 37:25.
[5] See Hebrews 4:15.
[6] Psalm 46:1.
[7] Genesis 21:17 NIV.
[8] Jeremiah 32:38-40.
[9] Habakkuk 2:3.
[10] Strong, "Hebrew and Chaldee Dictionary," s.v. "Beersheba," Gen. 21:14, entry #884, p. 18.
[11] Genesis 22:14: "Jehovah-jireh" (KJV) and THE-LORD-WILL-PROVIDE (NKJV).
[12] Philippians 4:13.
[13] Galatians 1:15.

[14] Jeremiah 1:5 NKJV.
[15] See Ephesians 3:20.
[16] Philippians 1:6.
[17] Jeremiah 1:12 AMP.
[18] See Philippians 2:13.
[19] Hebrews 10:23.
[20] See Revelation 1:18.
[21] 1 Corinthians 15:54.
[22] 1 Corinthians 15:55.
[23] See Romans 10:9.
[24] See Ecclesiastes 3:14,15; Psalm 33:11 NIV.

Chapter 4
[1] Exodus 16:15.
[2] See Exodus 13:21.
[3] Genesis 1:27.
[4] 1 Samuel 1:1,19.
[5] Judges 21:25.
[6] Hitchcock, Roswell D., *Hitchcock's Bible Name Dictionary*, "Entry for 'Elkanah,'" "An Interpreting Dictionary of Scripture Proper Names" by Roswell D. Hitchcock, New York, N.Y., 1869.
[7] 2 Corinthians 4:7 KJV.
[8] See 1 Samuel 1:3-5.
[9] See 1 Samuel 1:5.
[10] Mark 10:27.
[11] See Philippians 2:14; 1 Corinthians 10:10.
[12] See Romans 12:1,2.
[13] Matthew 12:34.
[14] See Jeremiah 1:12.
[15] John 15:7.
[16] See Mark 9:23.

Chapter 5
[1] Isaiah 1:18.
[2] John 3:30.
[3] Numbers 6:1-8.
[4] 2 Corinthians 5:7.
[5] Ecclesiastes 5:5.
[6] See 2 Corinthians 10:15.
[7] Matthew 9:29.
[8] Matthew 9:22.
[9] Proverbs 15:1 MESSAGE.
[10] Luke 3:5.
[11] Proverbs 3:6.
[12] Psalm 37:23.

[13] Revelation 13:8.

Chapter 6
[1] Ecclesiastes 1:9.
[2] Merrill F. Unger, ed. R.K. Harrison, *The New Unger's Bible Dictionary* (Chicago: Moody Press, Revised and Updated Edition, "Additional and New Material," 1988, The Moody Bible Institute of Chicago), s.v. "Abigail," p. 5.
[3] Psalm 139:14.
[4] Genesis 1:31.
[5] Genesis 2:18,20,24.
[6] 1 Samuel 16:11-13.
[7] 1 Samuel 25:1.
[8] 1 Samuel 16:14-23.
[9] 1 Samuel 17:50,51; 23:5.
[10] 1 Samuel 18:5-10.
[11] 1 Samuel 24:1-4.
[12] 1 Samuel 24:5-22.
[13] See 2 Timothy 2:23.

Chapter 7
[1] James 2:17.
[2] Psalm 33:11.
[3] Proverbs 15:1.

Chapter 8
[1] Revelation 12:11.
[2] Proverbs 18:16.
[3] See Joshua 14:6-14.
[4] Philippians 2:8.

Chapter 9
[1] 2 Corinthians 1:20.
[2] Mark 11:24.
[3] Ephesians 2:6.
[4] Isaiah 28:16; Romans 9:33; 10:11; 1 Peter 2:6.

Chapter 10
[1] See Exodus 3:10.
[2] Proverbs 18:21.
[3] Psalm 89:33.
[4] Acts 10:34.
[5] 2 Samuel 22:8.
[6] Psalm 136:13.
[7] Joshua 10:13.
[8] Jeremiah 29:11.
[9] Hebrews 11:6.

Chapter 11

[1] Hitchcock, Roswell D. "Entry for 'Tirzah.'" "An Interpreting Dictionary of Scripture Proper Names." <http://www.studylight.org/dic/hbn/view.cgi?number=T2464>. New York, N.Y., 1869.

[2] Numbers 16:1,2.

[3] 1 Corinthians 12:13.

[4] James 4:2.

[5] "...if you have faith as a mustard seed, you will say to this mountain, 'Move from here to there,' and it will move; and nothing will be impossible for you" (Matt. 17:20).

Chapter 12

[1] 1 Timothy 6:12.

[2] John 11:42.

[3] Deuteronomy 4:40.

[4] 1 Chronicles 4:10.

[5] Psalm 86:17.

[6] See Deuteronomy 1:35.

Chapter 13

[1] Judges 4:1-3.

[2] Psalm 46:1.

[3] Psalm 121:2.

[4] 2 Peter 1:3.

[5] See Mark 11:24.

[6] Philippians 1:6.

Chapter 15

[1] Proverbs 15:33.

[2] Judges 5.

[3] Proverbs 4:23.

Chapter 16

[1] Exodus 16:35.

[2] Deuteronomy 31:16.

[3] Exodus 33:19.

Chapter 17

[1] Deuteronomy 30:15.

[2] Proverbs 3:5.

[3] Hebrews 13:5.

[4] Hebrews 12:2.

[5] Psalm 35:27.

[6] Ezekiel 12:28.

[7] Deuteronomy 28:2.

[8] Isaiah 1:19.

[9] Hebrews 11:6.

Chapter 18
[1] Psalm 84:11.
[2] 2 Corinthians 5:17.
[3] Romans 4:22.
[4] Hebrews 11:6.
[5] Isaiah 55:11.
[6] See Matthew 1 (esp. verse 5).
[7] See Matthew 1:5-16.
[8] 2 Corinthians 5:17.

Chapter 19
[1] Esther 2:7.
[2] Esther 2:7.
[3] Philippians 2:7; Matthew 16:21.
[4] T. Megillah, 13a.
[5] Esther 2:10.
[6] Esther 2:11.
[7] Esther 2:12.
[8] 1 Corinthians 13:12.

Chapter 20
[1] See John 4:34.
[2] Henry H. Halley, *Halley's Bible Handbook* (Grand Rapids, Zondervan, 1965) p. 688.
[3] Esther 2:16.

Chapter 21
[1] See Esther 1:11-19.
[2] Esther 2:19-23.
[3] Esther 3:1-2.
[4] Esther 3:2-6.
[5] Esther 3:8-11.
[6] Esther 4:1.
[7] Esther 4:5-8.
[8] See Psalm 21:4.
[9] Philippians 2:8.
[10] Psalm 37:4,5.
[11] Psalm 84:11.
[12] Colossians 2:15.
[13] Matthew 16:19.
[14] Psalm 2:8.
[15] Philippians 4:6-8.
[16] Psalm 121:1,2.
[17] Esther 7:1-8:2.

Prayer of Salvation

God loves you—no matter who you are, no matter what your past. God loves you so much that He gave His one and only begotten Son for you. The Bible tells us that "...whoever believes in Him should not perish but have everlasting life" (John 3:16 NKJV). Jesus laid down His life and rose again so that we could spend eternity with Him in heaven and experience His absolute best on earth. If you would like to receive Jesus into your life, say the following prayer out loud and mean it from your heart.

Heavenly Father, I come to You admitting that I am a sinner. Right now, I choose to turn away from sin, and I ask You to cleanse me of all unrighteousness. I believe that Your Son, Jesus, died on the cross to take away my sins. I also believe that He rose again from the dead so that I might be forgiven of my sins and made righteous through faith in Him. I call upon the name of Jesus Christ to be the Savior and Lord of my life. Jesus, I choose to follow You and ask that You fill me with the power of the Holy Spirit. I declare that right now I am a child of God. I am free from sin and full of the righteousness of God. I am saved in Jesus' name. Amen.

If you prayed this prayer to receive Jesus Christ as your Savior for the first time, please contact us on the Web at **www.harrison-house.com** to receive a free book.

Or you may write to us at
Harrison House
P.O. Box 35035
Tulsa, Oklahoma 74153

About the Author

The ministry of Dr. Pat Bailey has created tremendous impact for more than 20 years in over 80 countries around the world, bringing deliverance and salvation to thousands. A 1982 graduate of New Life Bible College in Tennessee, a 1984 charter class graduate of Victory World Missions Training Center in Tulsa, Oklahoma, and a 1993 graduate of All Nations for Christ Bible Institute in Benin City, Nigeria, Patricia D. Bailey's journey into ministry began at the age of 21 with an invitation from the late Daisy Osborn (wife of T. L. Osborn) to travel to East and West Africa.

Dr. Bailey is a lecturer, author, and founder of Master's Touch Ministries International, a mission outreach. MTM has also founded Y.U.G.O. (Young Adults United for Global Outreach) and Sister to Sister, an international outreach to women in foreign countries. Dr. Bailey serves as a missions strategy consultant to several growing churches and has developed leadership programs around the world.

Dr. Bailey has focused her recent efforts of spreading the liberating good news of the Gospel of Jesus Christ toward the people living in the 10/40 window, which includes North Africa and the Middle East, the most populated but least evangelized area in the world. She concentrates much of her ministry to a group of people who have no voice—refuges, widows, and orphans.

Dr. Bailey's school of missions, which she launched in early 2004, is training nationals to return to their nations. In the first six months of existence, the nationals will have reached the number of nations Dr. Bailey has personally ministered in her more than two decades of ministry.

Master's Touch Ministries has headquarters in Atlanta, Los Angeles, and London. Dr. Bailey is the proud mother of a son, Karim Israel Bailey.

*Royalties from the sale of this book will go towards the
Master's Touch Ministries Widows and Orphans Outreach.*

To contact Dr. Bailey, please write:

Dr. Patricia D. Bailey
Master's Touch Ministries International
P.O. Box 3175
Alpharetta, Georgia 30023
Web site: www.mtmintl.org

*Please include your prayer requests
and comments when you write.*

Also Available by Patricia D. Bailey

Step Into Divine Destiny

Additional copies of this book
are available from your local bookstore.

www.harrisonhouse.com

Fast. Easy. Convenient!

- ◆ New Book Information
- ◆ Look Inside the Book
- ◆ Press Releases
- ◆ Bestsellers

- ◆ Free E-News
- ◆ Author Biographies
- ◆ Upcoming Books
- ◆ Share Your Testimony

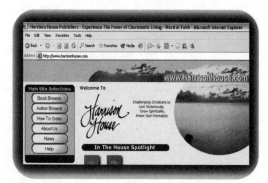

For the latest in book news and author information, please visit us on the Web at www.harrisonhouse.com. Get up-to-date pictures and details on all our powerful and life-changing products. Sign up for our e-mail newsletter, *Friends of the House,* and receive free monthly information on our authors and products including testimonials, author announcements, and more!

Harrison House—
Books That Bring Hope, Books That Bring Change

The Harrison House Vision

Proclaiming the truth and the power
Of the Gospel of Jesus Christ
With excellence;

Challenging Christians to
Live victoriously,
Grow spiritually,
Know God intimately.